One of the colourful L.O.R. posters of the era when the North-end docks were used mainly by passenger ships.

Seventeen Stations to Dingle

The Liverpool Overhead Railway

remembered by

John W. Gahan

Published jointly by:

Countyvise

1 & 3 Grove Road, Rock Ferry, Birkenhead,
Merseyside. L42 3XS.

ISBN 0 907768 20 2

and

AVON-ANGLIA

Publications & Services, Annesley House, 21 Southside,
Weston-Super-Mare, Avon. BS23 2QU.

ISBN 0 905466 54 3

*Printed in England by: BIRKENHEAD PRESS LTD.,
1 & 3 Grove Road, Rock Ferry, Birkenhead, Merseyside. L42 3XS.*

To the memory
of the late
Walter M. Purdey.

FOREWORD

The 30th December, 1981 marked the 25th Anniversary of the closure of the Liverpool Overhead Railway, an event still deeply lamented in many Liverpool hearts. With this in mind I felt that it would be fitting to recall the occasion with a commemorative booklet dealing with the railway, not a history but an evocative recollection of the line in its heyday.

For the sake of completeness the essential basic historical facts and dates have been included, together with some notes on the rolling stock, tickets, publicity etc. A thorough and comprehensive history of the Overhead Railway was written shortly after its closure by Mr. C.E. Box, and this remains the definitive work on the subject. This essay complements the earlier work in recalling the sights and sounds of the "Overhead", in the hope that it will appeal to those citizens who recall the railway, as well as the numerous railway enthusiasts.

The "Overhead" was a well-loved Liverpool institution and it has been a pleasantly nostalgic task to add my own memories and notes on the railway to the growing literature on Liverpool's not altogether tranquil, but nonetheless wonderful and fascinating past.

Liverpool.
December, 1981.

Map of the Liverpool overhead Railway. By courtesy of the Railway Magazine.

The Dockers Umbrella.

From Seaforth Sands to Dingle,
a lengthy metal span,
traversed the land of docks and quays,
through which the trains once ran.

The "Overhead", *our* railway,
known to one and all,
Served the docks and river front,
a wondrous place withal.

To work in early morning,
or coming home at night,
the crowds flocked to the stations,
every train packed tight.

They gazed upon the shipping,
a wondrous sight to all,
for ships of every nation,
made this a port of call.

The metal spans of bridgework,
the busy streets below,
the homely, friendly stations,
the shining rails aglow.

Wapping, Clarence, Gladstone Docks,
these and many more,
harboured the ships of commerce,
along the Mersey shore.

The world-wide names of shipping lines,
lettered on dock walls,
the engines, cranes and pigeons,
the many siren calls.

Streets of varied buildings,
ware-houses vast and high,
filled the mind with wonder,
as the busy trains passed by.

The men of many nations,
those of Liverpool too,
rode the trains together,
a cheery, happy crew!

Since the railway vanished,
with no vestigial trace,
the great dock-land of Liverpool,
is a less inviting place!

JWG.

A train of modernised rolling stock at Seaforth Sands station. August, 1955.   Photo J.B. Horne.

The Liverpool Overhead Railway, 1893-1956.

Throughout 63 busy years, the Liverpool Overhead Railway was both a useful asset and a landmark to the residents of Merseyside. Indeed, it was not possible to reach the famous Pier Head, venue of the river ferries and ocean liners, or any of the docks that stretch along the Mersey shore without first passing beneath the red-leaded bridgework of that unique transport undertaking which straddled and cast its shadow almost the entire length of the main road that runs parallel with the river for a distance of more than six miles. The structure that formed this lengthy land bridge resembled a many legged monster, an impression created by the hundreds of girders and stanchions that carried the rails sixteen feet above the ground. There must hardly be an elder citizen who does not recall with acute nostalgia his or her early memories of the Overhead Railway as, when travelling to the Pier Head on a tram, or when walking along James Street, Water Street or Chapel Street, the railway was the first feature to catch the eye. This was so despite the presence of the three enormous buildings — the Dock Office, Cunard, and Royal Liver, which tower high above the streets and dominate the skyline in that fascinating locality. The trams passed through a crowded commercial district on the last stage of their inward journeys, and upon reaching the dock road, the Overhead Railway sprang suddenly into view, with the wide River Mersey and its shipping forming the background. Here indeed was the gateway to adventure excitingly displayed before the gaze of young and old — a scene that was continually thrilling and ever full of interest.

In order to reach their many-tracked terminus at the busy Pier Head just behind the great landing stage, the trams actually crossed two railways at one and the same time in a strange place to find railways at all — in the commercial streets of a great city. Their steel wheels pounded over the shiny manganese right-angled crossings by means of which the rails of the tramways intersected those of the goods railway line that served the docks, whilst their trolleys struck blue flashes from the copper wires that were suspended on insulators fixed to the bridge decking of the Overhead Railway. Eye-catching gilt lettering applied to the structure's girders boldly advertised several well-known local ales, whilst colourful posters showing a lovely blue Mersey full of ships exhorted people to see the docks and liners by taking a round-trip ticket on the line, at a remarkably cheap fare.

The immensely fascinating Liverpool Overhead Railway was familiar not only to regular workers along the Mersey shoreline, but also to a multitude of others, citizens and visitors alike, people not only from all parts of Britain but also from far flung places of the

Earth. The "Overhead" as it was usually termed, was known from Rangoon to San Francisco and from Greenland to Australia as one of the most notable institutions of the great port of Liverpool, and most of the sailors whose ships moored along the Mersey travelled on it between dockside and city centre on the first stage of a journey home to some other town, or when returning to their ships to commence another voyage to a distant port. Others rode to and from the city in quest of entertainment and glamorous company, to make their short stay in Liverpool more congenial.

At some obscure date in the past the Overhead Railway acquired a secondary title by which it was often referred to by the men who worked along the river front. It was christened the "Docker's Umbrella" by some dockland comedian — quite appropriately, as the sheltering bridgework was much appreciated by people who had to walk along the dock road during heavy rain. In harder, leaner times which Liverpool has known in full measure, men without resources to cover the cost of a night's lodging sought shelter and actually slept on the hard granite setts beneath the structure, and crews of early morning goods trains had to be sure the track was clear of recumbent bodies as they made their way along in Winter's darkness! The "umbrella" developed many leaks in later years due to a variety of causes, but this belongs to the other end of the story. A new era in Liverpool transport was to begin when the "Overhead" was ceremonially opened in the final decade of the Victorian era and commenced a long and useful career in the service of Merseyside's population.

Origin and Promotion of the "Overhead" Railway.

As the port of Liverpool expanded in size and its shipping traffic increased during the middle and latter years of the nineteenth century, the vehicular and foot traffic on the long road that served the dock estate increased likewise until problems and confusion threatened to strangle business and movement. Along that road continuous wheeled traffic passed to and fro. Large, heavily laden lorries and drays, timber transporters and other big vehicles hauled by herculean horses forged their way through the throng of carriages, cabs and omnibuses, whilst hundreds of carts and barrows were pushed by men and boys, all jostling for road space, so it was small wonder that the salt-sea air was often split by streams of picturesque invective and argument. Carriage owners — the merchants, brokers and ship-owners found themselves subjected to long delays and suffered slow, frustrated journeys along the docks, so that some of them resorted to walking rather than participate in the worsening traffic struggle. Repeated demands for something to be done in the way of improvement had no effect, much talk and no action being the rule for many years.

By the late 1840's the docks extended for a distance of approximately three miles, from Wellington Dock at the North end of the town to Brunswick Dock at the South end, and the need for speedy passenger transport free of the teeming commercial traffic was beginning to be felt in earnest. By the year 1852 rails for merchandise traffic had been laid along the stone-setted dock road, with branches diverging to penetrate docks, sheds, works and warehouses, but for many years the railway wagons were hauled by horses because the dock authorities would not permit the use of steam locomotives owing to the risk of fire among the sheds and cargoes. Sailing ships still dominated the dockland scene but tall, thin funnels were beginning to appear among the forests of masts and spars, and little was it realised at that time that the much revered sailing ships with their acres of billowing canvas were doomed to gradual extinction as thrusting connecting rods and churning paddle wheels driven by tireless steam took over sea transport. The docks, streets and warehouses were populated by tough, bearded men who perforce took hard work and long hours in their stride and endured considerable hardship in their daily tasks. Especially was this so of the seafarers, for those picturesque ships at rest so peacefully in the calm waters of the enclosed docks exacted unceasing toil from their hardy crews on their lengthy voyages, though in spite of such rough living and working conditions, a fierce loyalty and love for the sea was characteristic of the men who formed their crews.

During the 1850's an inventive gentlemen named W.H. Curtiss of London visited Liverpool and soon noticed the dockland travel problems — he also noticed the presence of the dockside goods railway and saw the possibility of using it for passenger traffic, not with trains, but with modified road omnibuses. He devised an arrangement of retractable flanges which, operated by a lever could be brought against the backs of the ordinary road wheels and thus enable the omnibuses to run on the rails. It was quite an ingenious scheme, which worked well in practice. Curtiss managed to obtain permission from the port authorities to operate his omnibuses and he introduced a service which became extremely popular. This commenced in 1859 and appeared to have a promising future. By running his omnibuses on the rails, they were segregated from other road traffic, but when catching up with a goods train (usually one or two wagons hauled by horses) they had to pull off the rails and overtake by rattling over the granite setts, regaining the rails further ahead. Curtiss was later obliged to pay tolls for the use of the railway, and eventually gave up the service but other omnibus operators came and pursued the practice of running on the rails. By the 1880's there was a very frequent service of these omnibuses, running at five-minute intervals during the business day. Regulations required that no omnibus must approach within 300 yeards of that preceding it, a regulation that was extremely difficult to observe, and increasing goods traffic meant that more and more trains got in the way. The Mersey Docks & Harbour Board increased the tolls but still the omnibus proprietors continued the service for many years, possibly until the Overhead Railway commenced to operate. No doubt the MD & HB were pleased to see the end of them so that the railway could revert to its original purpose, that of a goods traffic only system.

In their heyday the horse-buses carried over two million passengers annually, but were far from being a satisfactory means of transport. There was still the need for some means of travel capable of providing a fast service of a kind well beyond the capacity of horse haulage, and this had been realised at an even earlier date than that on which Curtiss introduced his omnibus. Indeed, in 1852 John Grantham, a notable engineer of the time proposed the construction of an elevated railway between Huskisson Dock (the newest then) and the Mersey Forge, Toxteth, a distance of four miles. The line was to have been supported on columns, 20 feet above the roadway, with the space below the decking used for the storage of merchandise. The railway was to have consisted of six tracks, and although a great deal of interest was shown in the scheme, nothing was actually done to put it into effect. Similar schemes were aired from time to time during the following years, again without any tangible results. In 1877 the Mersey Docks & Harbour Board, the governing body of the docks, having become accutely concerned about the dock road traffic situation, proposed to construct an elevated railway. They also gave consideration to an underground line as an alternative but the latter found no favour owing to the probable heavy cost and the difficulties of constructing such a railway through the complex dockland. Mr. George Lyster, M.Inst., C.E., of the MD & HB voyaged to New York in order to study the already well established elevated railways in that city, which was the first to exploit them, and upon his return home drew up plans for an elevated line along the Liverpool waterfront.

Lyster planned a double track system, but not everybody concerned in the scheme considered that double track was necessary, notably Alfred Holt, M.Inst.C.E., who was a member of the Dock Board. He, and some others were of the opinion that a single track railway with passing loops at each station would meet the purpose and he found such support that the MD & HB applied for Parliamentary Powers to build the line in this form, the Act being passed in 1878. As was the practice on the New York elevated railroads, the trains were intended to be hauled by steam locomotives, but not without many misgivings because of the potential fire hazard from sparks thrown out of the chimneys of hard-working locomotives showering down on the streets and wharves.

The Board of Trade, upon examining the plans for the single line railway, condemned it forthwith, having realised that in the ever growing port, traffic would increase to an extent that would soon overwhelm the capacity of the proposed line and fresh problems would be created. Such a system would have been somewhat akin to the horse tramways on the streets so far as operational convenience was concerned, and it seems incredible that only a few persons connected with the enterprise had sufficient perspicacity to see that a double track line was essential. The result of the Board of Trade report was a halt to any further progress, and the subject of a railway along the docks remained in abeyance for a further length of time.

Lyster, the Docks Engineer kept the railway scheme alive, and worked on a report which he presented to the Mersey Docks & Harbour Board in 1882. This report dealt with the course the proposed line would follow and the possible effects that its construction would have on the dock road and goods railway traffic etc. The Board, satisfied with the revised scheme applied for new Powers, which were duly granted, but they made no move towards constructing the railway, mainly because some members considered that railway lines for carrying passengers were outside the scope of their activities. At last however, in 1888, when the docks stretched from Toxteth in the South to Alexandra at the North end of the city, Sir William B. Forwood and other leading citizens formed the Liverpool Overhead Railway Company to construct what, in the ponderous terminology of the times was called "a line of rails along the docks". The Parliamentary Powers held by the Mersey Docks & Harbour Board were thereupon transferred to the railway company by an Act of 24th July, 1888.

The Chairman of the Liverpool Overhead Railway Company, Sir William Forwood, was one of the bygone giants of the City Council. He was born in January, 1840, when railways were still new, and lived to see electric traction developed. He was a man of immense energy and enterprise, was widely travelled and was connected with many milestones in the progress of the city. After a long career of sterling municipal service, Sir William Forwood became the "Grand Old Man" of the Liverpool Council, and continued his unflagging interest in the city and its affairs until his death in 1928 at the age of 88 years. His fellow directors in the new railway venture were mainly men concerned with commerce and shipping.

We have already noted that streets in Far-off New York were overshadowed by elevated railroads, the first one being opened in the year 1872. Upon these spidery-looking structures trains composed of wooden cars with open platforms either end were hauled by sturdy 0-4-4 Tank locomotives of a design specially developed for local and suburban passenger traffic by the American engineer Matthias N. Forney, by whose name these particular locomotives became known throughout the railway world. They were also extensively used in Chicago and elsewhere in the United States. Those engaged on planning the new Liverpool line took particular note of the construction and operating methods of the New York railroads, but did not follow their design so far as the structure was concerned, not favouring the high, open trestle-work, sometimes minus sides or guard railings, and openwork flooring. The Liverpool Overhead Railway structure subsequently built was a model of its kind as the result of extra careful design and a regard for aesthetic qualities, and there was no possibility of red-hot cinders falling into the streets from the ashpans of hard-worked locomotives because the structure was completely floored. Ash removal would have posed a problem however, had steam operation actually materialised.

Little did the promoters of the Liverpool Overhead Railway realise what they would be up against when it came to the actual construction of the line. The route had to be very carefully planned in order to thread its way through a complex area along the waterfront consisting of docks, roads, railways, sheds and warehouses. Anything that lay in the path of the structure such as police and customs buildings etc., had to be demolished and new ones built elsewhere. By order of the Mersey Docks & Harbour Board, the dockside railway had to be realigned in certain places and the cost of this work alone amounted to £60,000 — quite a large amount of money in those days. The supporting columns had to be sunk into the walls of dockside sheds and warehouses in many instances, and no interference with traffic on either the dock road or railway was allowed while the work was in progress. The original plan had been to take the line inland in the Pier Head area, along The Strand at the rear of the huge colonaded warehouses known as The Goree Piazzas, but the Liverpool Health Committee, whose jurisdiction extended to transport would not permit this to be done. Presumably the railway might have offended the eyes of the merchants and businessmen looking out of their office windows in this dignified commercial area of the city. No! the railway had to be kept strictly in its place, along the waterfront. The Health Committee, in granting the company leave to move a column a few inches outside the Parliamentary limits, required the re-paving of Wapping at a cost of £8,000. These, together with many other restrictions and problems had to be overcome, and on looking back it seems a miracle that the railway was ever built at all! The promoters took it all in their stride however, and pressed ahead with the construction, which unfortunately could not be completed within the time specified in the Act of 1888, so a new Act was obtained which allowed a further three years in which to finish the work.

The rapid development of electric traction on passenger-carrying railways and street-car lines in the United States of America led the company to consider abandoning the proposal for steam operation, but no definite decision on this matter was taken until 1891, in which year the City & South London Railway was opened — a tube line which employed electric locomotives. The only other examples of new-fangled electric traction in the British Isles at that date were the Blackpool tramways, the Giant's Causeway tramway in Ireland and Magnus Volk's railway at Brighton. Although successful, these small systems did not transport the enormous numbers of passengers that the Liverpool line was likely to do.

The final decision to electrify the Liverpool Overhead Railway appears to have been due to the efforts of Forwood and Lyster. This decision was not devoid of risk however, as electric traction was still a new thing and the company had no means of knowing whether it would prove to be successful, financially or operationally. In addition, people were inclined to fear electricity, and even after the railway was opened a trip on it was looked upon with trepidation by timid persons. This fear was also manifest among passengers on the early electric trams, especially when flashing and arcing occurred at the trolley and wheels, which was akin to lightning to the uninitiated. There were however, some bolder people who were immensely intrigued by the idea of lightning-impelled vehicles. The remarkable efficiency of electric traction and its safe operation once the line had commenced to run soon dispelled all fears and passengers began to enjoy the novel experience of riding in clean, fast "locomotiveless"

15

trains. Liverpool was one of the pioneer cities to employ electric traction on a railway, and when the "Overhead" began to operate the trams were still horse-drawn and the neighbouring Mersey Railway was still an all-steam line. Seafaring men from remoter lands were immensely impressed when, upon seeking transport from the docks to the city, they were directed to the wonderful new mode of conveyance and were duly puzzled by its mysteries.

Sailors from all parts of the World found Liverpool to be a place of magic in more ways than one and the new electric railway served to prove the point. At that time it was a city teeming with life and continuous activity, with a great river at its doorstep, miles of busy docks and wharves and an air of commercial urgency as the populace went about its daily work. It was a city ruled by merchants, brokers and shipowners, whose offices with their polished brass nameplates on their portals loomed over the streets through which passed an unceasing flow of traffic. The beating of hooves and the clang of tramcar gongs were the sounds of transportation into which the new electric railway struck a revolutionary note.

We have leapt ahead a little in the forgoing and must return to the time when the Liverpool Overhead Railway was still the unrealised ambition of its promoters. Raising capital, often a major hurdle in any new venture proved an easy matter, there being plenty of subscribers to such a promising project. The head office of the company was established at No.31 James Street, within short walking distance of the railway-to-be, and the Act of Parliament for its construction having been secured, the forces were marshalled to put the immensely complex task in operation. The Contractor engaged for carrying out the project was J.W. Willans of Manchester.

An L.O.R. advertisement from the year 1926.

Save Time
Save Money

THE

OVERHEAD

IS STILL THE CHEAPEST TRANSPORT

TO THE CITY

Study these Fares

DINGLE to PIER HEAD	THIRD CLASS	
	$3\tfrac{1}{2}$D SINGLE	$6\tfrac{1}{2}$D RETURN

Season Tickets - Unlimited Journeys

DINGLE to PIER HEAD	THIRD CLASS	
	WEEKLY	MONTHLY
	4/3	16/3

First Class Extra   -   -   -   -   Children Reduced Fares

FREQUENT & PUNCTUAL SERVICE

Travelling on the "overhead" was inexpensive in 1955.

Construction of the Railway.

The decision was made to commence work at the North end of the docks and a base was therefore established in a part of the North Mersey goods yard of the Lancashire & Yorkshire Railway in October, 1889. Here the individual bridge spans were assembled complete, ready to be transported to their intended positions on the columns being erected ahead of them along the dock road. Forges, presses and rivetting machines were installed at the base, which became a busy and noisy hive of activity when the work had begun. Millions of red-hot rivets were hammered into place as the wagonloads of metal sections arrived continuously from the Hamilton Ironworks at Garston, at which they were manufactured.

The structure of the railway, which was designd jointly by two of the most prominent engineers of the period — Sir Douglas Fox and J.H. Greathead, consisted of a series of wrought-iron girders placed at a distance of 22 feet, centre to centre, supported on columns built up from steel plates and girders with a normal span of 50 feet. The normal height of the railway track was 16 feet above the roadway but this was varied, and so was the span in a large number of special instances where circumstances required it. Bowstring girder bridges with a maximum span of 98 feet were provided at places where the railway crossed wide thoroughfares, there being four such bridges — one at James Street and two, a short distance apart, at St. Nicholas Place in Liverpool, also one near Seaforth Sands on a subsequent extension of the line. The actual decking on which the track was laid took the form of strong arched steel plates, a novel type of flooring designed by G.L. Hobson. The rails, of flat-bottomed section were laid on longitudinal timbers affixed to the decking, thus the track presented a rather strange, bare appearance, especially as it was not ballasted. It resembled in some ways the early broad gauge permanent way of the Great Western Railway in the days of the great engineer Isambard Kingdom Brunel.

In order to permit high loads to enter or leave the dock estate provision had to be made for certain of the spans to lift (by hydraulic power) and such lifting sections were provided at Brunswick, Sandon and Langton Docks. At Stanley Dock it was necessary to provide facilities for ships to pass beneath the railway because this particular dock was situated on the landward side of the line, and connection was made via the dock with the Leeds & Liverpool Canal. An early bridge carrying the road and dock railway had to be replaced by a structure carrying the overhead Railway also, and the opportunity was taken to install a combined lifting and swing bridge, with the road and docks railway on the lower lifting section and the new Overhead Railway on the upper level. The lower spans could be raised to allow smaller vessels through without interference to the upper section, but to allow large ships to pass, the whole bridge had to be swung open. The Brunswick, Sandon and Langton lift bridges were operated only during the night after the last train had passed. In later years a separate lifting type road bridge was provided alongside the railway bridge at Stanley Dock.

The first section of the railway to be built spanned the five or so miles between Alexandra Dock and Herculaneum Dock via the Pier Head. The difficulties presented through the no-interference to traffic on the dock road rule were overcome in an ingenious manner. Construction commenced with the erection of a short length of bridgework at North Mersey in the normal manner, thereafter a special technique was applied. Each succeeding span, upon completion at the base was transported to the site and hoisted onto the already completed length of structure, then placed on a trolley on which it was hauled to its intended location. The trolley was pulled along by horses working on the roadway, but eventually a kind of steam tractor was devised which ran on the rails which were quickly laid as each span was completed. On the arrival at the end of the line as it had thus far progressed, each new span was picked up by cranes mounted upon a movable gantry devised by Edward William Ives. This special gantry was mounted on four legs — two long and two short, the former running on rails laid temporarily on the roadway, and the latter running on the outer rails of the track already laid on the completed portion of the structure. After the cranes had taken hold of the new span, the gantry was moved forward and the span next lowered and fixed onto the previously built columns. There were some sections on which this method could not be employed however, mainly where the spans had to be placed closely against warehouse walls. At such places the columns had to be sunk into the brickwork of these buildings.

The efficient and speedy method of constructing the Overhead Railway aroused considerable interest in engineering circles and many professionals and other interested parties journeyed to Liverpool to observe the work in progress. Upon completion a total of 567 spans had gone into the structure, so the magnitude of the task can be well appreciated. The railway was by no means a straight one, as one-sixth of its length was on curves, some of them so severe that they imposed a restriction upon the length of the carriages that formed the trains.

The railway structure was of neat and pleasing design, being completely devoid of the florid, ornamental ironwork that was so beloved of the Victorian designers as exemplified by some of the station architecture on the Paris Metro or the Chicago elevated systems. Indeed, the appearance of it was so neat that it did not become "dated" for many years and still presented a pleasing picture in later days when we had become used to the clean designs of steel and concrete bridges. The disadvantage was the continual need for painting and other necessary precautions against the destructive industrial atmosphere and the weather, both of which eventually gained the upper hand and sealed the doom of the railway after 60 years of service.

At Bramley-Moore Dock the railway had to descend to street level in order to pass beneath the L & Y branch railway to the coal tips that had been installed as long ago as 1855. On this section, known to the LOR staff as the "switchback" after the popular fairground attraction, the rails were laid in the normal manner on transverse timber sleepers and stone-ballasted. The gradient on this section was at 1 in 40, and traversing it was a great thrill for the younger passengers, especially as it was the only place on the entire railway where a train passed under a bridge. The docks railway was diverted to the riverward side of the LOR here, as it could not run beneath it, of course. Massive stone walls divided the Overhead Railway and the dock estate from the public roadway at this location, where the date 1844 could be seen cut into the stonework of the fortress-like walls. The Bramley-Moore Dock was named after a former Chairman of the Docks Committee.

By early 1893 the first section of the Liverpool Overhead Railway was complete and rolling stock was arriving, the vehicles being transported on road wagons hauled by steam traction engines. They were off-loaded and placed on the rails at the centre of the "switchback" where the track was at street level. On 4th February, 1893 the railway was formally opened by the Marquis of Salisbury, who switched on the power at the company's new generating station at Bramley-Moore, and then travelled over the line in a special train, of which one of the carriages had been fitted up in an elegant manner with movable chairs and potted plants! Public services commenced on 6th March, 1893 and the railway soon became a useful and popular addition to the transport facilities of Liverpool, though there were a few sceptics who prophesied its early doom or financial ruin.

Although the new railway carried plenty of passengers during the working day, it saw little traffic in the evenings after the dock workers had gone home — mainly seafarers travelled after six o'clock, and it was obvious that extensions would have to be made to tap residential areas as soon as possible. In 1894 work was commenced on a Northward extension from Alexandra Dock to Seaforth Sands, where the railway's course alongside the river and docks was altered to curve inland to reach its new terminal station, and was thus able to serve the residential districts of Seaforth and nearby Waterloo. This extension was brought into use on 30th April, 1894. Another extension was next commenced at the Southern end of the line, also turning inland, crossing the dock Road and Cheshire Lines Railway on a steel lattice girder bridge with a span of 200 feet, the longest on the system, then plunging directly into a tunnel half-a-mile in length beneath the streets to bring it to the terminal station in Park Road, Dingle, adjacent to a large residential area. This tunnel crossed above, with limited clearance, the St. Michael's tunnel of the Cheshire Lines and special work in the way of reinforcement proved necessary at this location to safeguard the main-line tunnel.

Dingle station was reached from the roadway by means of stairs and a subway — a real puzzle to any strangers who may have been advised to take the train to town as they would have the novel experience of proceeding underground to board an overhead train! This was just one more of the many unusual features of this railway of surprises. The Dingle extension was opened on 21st December, 1896. Competition loomed on the horizon however, as the first line of the Liverpool Corporation Tramways to be electrified was the one between Dingle and South Castle Street in the city, parallelling the Overhead Railway. Railway and tramway were about a quarter of a mile apart for the whole distance, the trams even terminating only a short distance from the Dingle railway station. Indeed, there was a tram stop outside the station. A curiosity here was the affixing of a gas lamp to an electric tramway standard — this was almost opposite the station entrance. The electric trams commenced operation on this route on 16th November, 1898 and took many passengers from the railway, mainly those living along Mill Street, St. James Street and Park Lane, because the tram route served the shopping streets and terminated at the foot of Lord Street in the city, whereas the railway followed the dock road and, in town, served only the commercial district. The same thing was to happen between Seaforth and town a short time later due to electrification of the tramways.

The original terminus station at Herculaneum Dock was replaced by a carriage shed when the Dingle extension was opened, the junction giving access to the new line being situated a little way to the North of the former terminus, and a new station was built at the Liverpool end of the junction. The passenger approach to this station was via a long, high iron footbridge from Grafton Street, crossing the yards of the Cheshire Lines Railway and the dock road. Only persons employed at, or having business at the docks were allowed to descend to the roadway here, in latter days at least, all others having to use the footbridge to gain the public streets. Incidentally, this footbridge was a fine vantage point for observing traffic on the busy Liverpool-Manchester main line of the C L C, the trains of which rushed by with engine whistles sounding shrilly as they passed the locomotive shed and yards where shunting of goods wagons was almost always in progress, whilst trains passed to and from the dock estate via rails laid across Sefton Street, which joined the MD & HB railway beneath the LOR viaduct.

The building of the Overhead Railway naturally gave rise to the possibility of Through train services between the South end of Liverpool, Seaforth, the resort of Southport, and Aintree (of racecourse fame), the potentialities of which seemed promising, and early in the new century the LOR and Lancashire & Yorkshire companies got together and formulated plans for such new facilities which could be accomplished with comparatively little effort and expense. The LOR station at Seaforth Sands was hard-by the L & Y goods line that ran between Aintree and the North Mersey yard. Near Seaforth & Litherland L & Y station empty land existed, which had once carried a connecting curve between the North Mersey Branch and the main Liverpool-Southport line, this connection having been removed some years previously, and the derelict embankment, which remained, was now given a new lease of useful life. A new embankment alongside that carrying the North Mersey Branch was constructed to link up with that of the old curve, and a new plate-girder bridge was built alongside the existing one spanning Crosby Road South, at Seaforth Sands. A double track, 46 chains in length, of main line construction using bull-head rails laid in chairs on transverse sleepers was provided for the extension and trains of the Liverpool Overhead Railway began to run through to Seaforth & Litherland L & Y station on 2nd July, 1905. A new station was built at Seaforth Sands alongside the original station there for the Through trains, but the older station was not demolished, being retained for trains terminating at this place. In 1906 a crossover was installed linking the new extension with the North Mersey Branch at Rimrose Road Junction, as it became known, a little way on the Seaforth side of Crosby Road bridge. A "standard" L & Y design signal box was built to control the junction, which enabled trains to be run between Dingle and Aintree via the LOR and L & Y lines.

The Dingle-Southport service commenced on 2nd February, 1906 with specially designed lightweight rolling stock built by the L & Y company, single-car trains being operated at first, later to be increased to two and three cars. From the Summer of 1906 an hourly service only was provided but as the project failed to bring the hoped-for traffic it was withdrawn in August, 1914. Thereafter passengers to and from Southport changed trains at Seaforth & Litherland L & Y station, which was the terminus for the LOR trains. The LOR used Running Powers over the L & Y between Seaforth Sands and Seaforth & Litherland, as the track belonged to the latter company.

The Dingle-Aintree service also commenced in 1906, again with the L & Y lightweight trains, an approximately hourly service being provided, later increased to half-hourly, but as in the case of the Southport service it did not pay its way and was discontinued as early as September, 1908. Both these services, operated by the L & Y company, involved the use of Running Powers over the Liverpool

Overhead Railway. The abandonment of the Aintree service left the crossover at Rimrose Road Junction without any regular traffic, but it was not removed, because twice a year special trains were provided between Dingle and Aintree on what was known as "Jump Sunday" and for the "Grand National" steeplechase the following Friday, on which the lightweight trains returned to the LOR scene from the Southport-Crossens line, on which they had worked since the Dingle to Southport and Aintree services ceased. The war of 1939-45 caused racing to be suspended (after the 1940 event) and the Rimrose Road crossover lay unused for seven years, acquiring a dull black coating of rust. In 1947 racing was resumed at Aintree, but the "Grand National" was altered to take place on a Saturday instead of Friday as previously, and only trains of LOR rolling stock made the through journeys due to the fact that the old L & Y trains had been scrapped in 1945, their replacements being too long and heavy for the Overhead Railway structure. Details of the race traffic will be given later.

When the railway was extended beyond Alexandra Dock, a workshop and carriage shed were built near the end of the line a little distance short of Seaforth Sands, and these remained in use until 1926, in which year a new and much larger depot and workshops were erected at the latter place, on the North side of Fort Road. These obliterated the original passenger station that had been in use since the line was extended to Seaforth Sands in 1894. The 1905 station, built for the Southport and Aintree trains and used only by trains to Seaforth & Litherland in subsequent years, began to handle both terminating and Through trains when the old station was closed, a crossover on the East side of Crosby Road South allowing trains to turn back.

The new workshops of 1926 had two levels — on the upper (railway) level repairs and overhaul of carriage bodies, also painting was carried out, whilst on the lower (street) level, work on bogies, wheels and electrical fittings was performed. A length of single track was provided on the lower level, which branched into two by means of a peculiar set of bladeless points. This track had no connection with the main line and was provided solely for the easy movement of carriage bogies, which were manhandled to the locations required.

The Liverpool Overhead Railway was the only example of its kind in Great Britain, and was the first such railway anywhere to be electrically operated. The New York lines, also those of Chicago, were subsequently electrified and the steam locomotives sold off to lumber mills and contractors all over the country, and many performed long years of trouble-free service amid scenes much different from the streets of their native cities.

When the Liverpool Overhead Railway was built the conductor rail was laid in the centre of each pair of running rails, but when the

Through working with the L & Y system was decided upon the live rail was removed to the outside of the running rails. Nevertheless, the centre rail was retained for earth-return purposes until 1921, when it was removed concurrently with a new signalling system, of which more later.

Electric current was supplied by the generating station at Bramley-Moore Dock, which was equipped with six Lancashire boilers, four steam horizontal engines and four dynamos, additional equipment being provided later for the extensions and also for the company's Crosby tramway, the latter which will be referred to again later. The generating station received coal direct from railway wagons, the bunkers being situated immediately beneath the high level line of the L & Y system that served the dockside coal tips from which many thousands of tons of coal were exported annually. An immensely fascinating place, the generating station remained in use until 1927 when it was closed down and current thereafter obtained more economically from the Liverpool Corporation Electric Supply Department. Closure of the generating station removed one of the Overhead Railway's most interesting features — the staff were extremely proud of the awe-inspiring array of machinery under their care, but much of the equipment dated from the earliest days of electric traction and was obsolete by the standards of the late 1920's.

Canada Dock Station, June, 1947. A train reversing direction on the emergency crossover. "Blitzed" goods yard and molasses tanks in the background.   *Photo N.N. Forbes.*

"Over the Overhead." A footbridge at Gladstone Dock station, photographed in June, 1949.

Photo N.N. Forbes.

A Southbound train ascending the incline at Bramley-Moore Dock, having passed beneath the ex L & Y branch to the dockside coal-tips. May, 1950.

Photo N.N. Forbes.

The junction of main and carriage shed lines at Seaforth Sands. A Cunard liner in Gladstone Dock is visible to the right of the train.

Photo L.O.R.

Canning station (formerly Custom House) photographed in 1952. Once a very busy station (until 1940 when the Custom House was destroyed by bombing), it was provided with better shelter than most of the other intermediate stations on the railway with the exception of Pier Head.

Photo R.B. Parr.

Herculaneum Dock station photographed in May, 1952. Note both colour-light and semaphore signals, the latter used for shunting purposes.

Photo R.B. Parr.

The Rolling Stock.

The trains which were supplied for working on the Liverpool Overhead Railway comprised an ultimate fleet of 19 three-carriage sets, of vehicles which were distinctive in design and totally unlike any other railway carriages in the whole of Britain — indeed, they embodied features of British, American and Continental practice rolled into one and were thus quite unique. The bodies were of timber, in matchboard pattern, resting on deep solebars. The roofs were of low-curved design, those on the motor units being curved downwards at the front end. The interiors were of the open or saloon type, with centre aisles and transverse seats placed back to back, of plain wood in the Third Class vehicles, leather-covered seats being provided in the First Class carriages. There were, at first, some composite carriages with both classes of accommodation but these were subsequently altered to Third Class. Decorated ceilings were a feature of the First Class vehicles, in comparison with the severely plain aspect of the Third Class with their white ceilings and brown ribbing, with varnished and buff-coloured woodwork. The plain aspect was relieved to some degree by advertisements in frames displayed on the end bulkheads, and a diagramatic map of the railway above the window level inside each carriage. It may be mentioned here that the designation Third Class did not apply until 1905, the accommodation being classed as Second before that year — it was altered in order to conform with L & Y Railway practice when Through operation was introduced. Fifty years later Third Class was altered to Second on the Nationalised British Railways system, but remained on the Liverpool Overhead.

Entry and exit to and from these remarkably individualistic carriages was made via hinged doors similar to those on the familiar compartment coaches on the main-line railways, but the LOR doors were so finely balanced that they would swing shut on their own when, as happened on occasions some tardy passenger leapt from the train at the last second after the right-away had been given and left the door open, but the jerk of the train starting-off would cause it to swing shut with absolute certainty. A visiting New Yorker on observing this remarked that the Liverpool Overhead Railway had the finest automatic doors he had ever seen! Through communication was provided throughout each train by means of end doors but there were no gangway connections. Railway staff only were permitted to pass from one carriage to another, and although many of the company's regulations were broken by its customers, this was one that was strictly observed.

The motor units of the first and second delivery of trains were equipped with one motor bogie only, with a single 60 horse-power motor. The third batch were slightly more powerful, the motor units having one 70 horse-power motor. From the year 1902 the trains were re-equipped and speeded-up to meet tramway competition, each motor unit being fitted with two 100 horse-power motorbogies. From 1919 onwards these motors were replaced by new design 75 horse-power motors. Spoked wheels were fitted to all bogies. The vehicles were connected to each other by an automatic coupling within a centrally-placed buffer, no side buffers being fitted.

It will have become apparent from the foregoing notes that the Liverpool Overhead trains were not exactly sumptuous in their appointments but very few complaints were made regarding the absence of luxury, in the Third Class at least (the First Class was not so bad at all). Generally, passengers on the "Overhead" did not worry much about wooden seats, as they were to be found on trams, buses and underground trains at one time, and indeed, they made a reappearance during World War 2 as, in order to save on materials, large numbers of new buses were fitted with them. They lasted long on the LOR however.

All the "Overhead" rolling stock was built, at intervals between 1892 and 1899, by Brown Marshall & Company, Ltd., of Birmingham, who later became the Metropolitan-Cammell Carriage, Wagon & Finance Company, Ltd. Electrical equipment was by the Electric Construction Company Ltd. There were differences in details between the various batches of trains and individual carriages, but except for length and width, they all latterly conformed to the same general pattern through successive alterations and rebuilding. Several motor units were rebuilt as trailers in the course of time. The majority of the carriages remained in use throughout the whole 63 year life span of the railway, and latterly were probably the oldest electric rail vehicles in service anywhere in the World. The livery was a somewhat sombre one of varnished brown, relieved by the crest of the company, a thin gilt line at waist level, gilt lettering and numerals, also a red panel with the carriage number in white on the front of each motor unit. The full title LIVERPOOL OVERHEAD RAILWAY COMPANY appeared either side of each vehicle. On the whole, the LOR trains were among the plainest ever to operate in Britain, but they possessed a character all of their own and were regarded with considerable affection by staff and passengers alike, whilst visitors to the city found them a great curiosity.

In the early days of the railway a service of single vehicles was sufficient for the off-peak periods but as traffic increased two, and later three-car trains became necessary throughout the day. The standard train for most of the life-span of the LOR consisted of two Third Class motor units with a First Class trailer placed between them, and a high-frequency service with such trains was needed to handle the passenger load, with extra trains during the peak traffic hours morning and evening.

The act of speeding up the trains following the electrification of the tramways resulted in the recapture of a great deal of traffic which was extremely pleasing, but the increase in speed and acceleration had an unfortunate debit side however, because the bridgework suffered as a result. In fact the structure had not only to absorb the immense strain of acceleration and deceleration of the trains and the thrust on the several curved sections, but corrosion from salty sea air, smoke and industrial acids also took their toll over the years, and constant attention was the price of keeping these unwelcome attackers from gaining the upper hand.

During the long period of the railway's life the trains ran ceaselessly to and fro on their countless journeys, carrying many millions of passengers on their dockland occasions, but by the time the second World war had ended they certainly looked, and felt their age! The excessive wear and tear of the war years, aggravated by shortages of materials for maintenance and renewal served to make continued operation of the old trains quite a headache.

In the year 1945 one or two carriages were partially modernised but the experiment of rebuilding a three-car train completely was decided upon and duly put in hand, a task that was finished in 1947, after which the train appeared in service and caused a minor sensation. The train concerned was formed of motor units Nos. 15 and 30, and trailer No. 7. In the rebuilding process the original underframe was retained, and so were the bogies, motors and control equipment, but the body of each carriage was completely revolutionised. Gone was the heavy timber construction and in its place was plywood and aluminium that gave a clean, up-to-date appearance. The seats in the Third Class carriages were now of comfortable leather, those in the First Class being of red moquette. Fittings were stainless steel and the hinged doors were replaced by power-operated sliding doors under control of the guard, which put an end to the antics of some of the more agile passengers of boarding and leaving the train whilst in motion. The staff quickly named the new train "The Streamliner", even though the traditional "square" look was still manifest and the train still unmistakably "Liverpool Overhead" in the same way that generations of London underground trains could not be mistaken for those of any other city. The dock workers were delighted with the new standard of comfort on what they regarded as their own railway, and many were the remarks and comments bandied about as the men rode to work in new luxury, and entered the train in an unaccustomed manner through the sliding doors. Liverpool wit reached new heights of expression, but the most frequently heard remark was "aren't we posh like"!

Splendid as the new train undoubtedly was, one feature struck dismay into the hearts of those passengers who did not play cards, read or doze on their journeys along the waterfront, but liked to survey the passing scene. The sad fact was that the windows were placed too high to enable a full view to be enjoyed without having to stand up, and the presence of longitudinal seats adjacent to the sliding doors did not help either, although the latter was unavoidable. The disadvantage of the high windows was soon remedied however, and further rebuilt carriages were provided with deeper windows that permitted a good view so that the company's main selling point to tourists, namely "See the Docks" was not lost. After all, colourful posters were displayed at the stations depicting the scenic aspect of the railway, which was its chief attraction for visitors to Liverpool, so that a good window layout was essential. This the old trains had in full measure.

In 1947 the company decided that a completely new fleet of trains was desirable, but investigations into the probable cost of re-equipping the railway in this manner revealed only too clearly that it was beyond their resources, and the decision was therefore taken to rebuild all the existing trains and bring them as up-to-date as possible. Between 1947 and 1955 six more trains were rebuilt, the work being carried out by a small group of men in the works at Seaforth Sands. The result of their craftsmanship and labour was extremely creditable, for the trains in their new form were the equal of any public service vehicles on Merseyside so far as good design and comfort were concerned. Alas however, an order to cease work was subsequently issued for reasons that will be outlined later.

The Stations.

A total of 17 stations served the docks and other important places along the route of the Overhead Railway proper, all except one being situated on the structure above the streets, and in general, each station consisted of an Up and Down platform on each of which was a timber-built waiting shelter. The ticket office at the Pier Head station was at street level, and so was that at Seaforth Sands, all other booking offices being at the head of the stairways at each station. At Dingle however, passengers obtained their tickets at an office situated at the street level, just inside the station entrance in Park Road. The name of each station appeared prominently in blue lettering on white enamelled metal signs, and station premises were liberally adorned with advertisements. Custom House station was somewhat superior to any other station that served the docks because it was provided with platform awnings, no doubt due to the fact that many "official" types boarded and alighted there, and perhaps saw more First Class passengers than any other intermediate station with the possible exception of the Pier Head.

Dingle station was entirely different from any other on the Overhead Railway because it was underground, well below street level! It consisted of an island platform, signal box and several sidings, all in a large whitewashed cavern hollowed out of the sandstone. No daylight penetrated Dingle station, which was permanently illuminated by electric lamps, and its situation suggested no possible connection with an "Overhead" railway.

Seaforth & Litherland station, at the opposite end of the line was built and owned by the Lancashire & Yorkshire Railway Company, and was situated on the Liverpool — Southport line. Four sets of rails passed through this station, which was on a high embankment, the facilities consisting of an island platform and one either side, making a total of four platform faces. It was an all-timber station, massively constructed, and stood in the heart of a large residential and partly industrial area. The LOR trains used the West side of the island platform, crossing from the Down relief to the Down main L & Y line to reach it, then departing in the opposite direction, gaining their own line, after a run of a few yards, at Seaforth South Junction. The approach to Seaforth & Litherland station was by means of the previously mentioned curve from West to North, on an embankment, the line having run closely beside the North Mersey goods line from Seaforth Sands. This section included Rimrose Road Junction crossover which connected the LOR and North Mersey lines, and was used only at the times that racing was held at Aintree. The junction signal box was normally opened only for these occasions, once a year, and the semaphore signal arms that governed the special train movements at this location were taken out of storage and affixed to the posts for a brief period of use and then removed and solemnly put away again for another year! Seaforth & Litherland station was the only place where LOR trains could normally be seen alongside main-line passenger rolling stock, except on "Grand National" day.

The trains that passed through Rimrose Road Junction crossover on race days traversed, between that junction and North Mersey Branch Junction (near Marsh Lane) track that was, as already noted, used by electric trains only twice a year up to 1940 and once a year in postwar years up to 1956, and the resultant brilliant arcing and spluttering from the collector shoes on the heavily rusted live rail were quite exciting! Between the latter junction and Aintree the line was used by main-line electric trains on a regular service between Liverpool Exchange and Aintree until 1951, and for a few years thereafter for empty stock workings so that the live rail was kept fairly free of heavy rusting and no extra-spectacular firework displays resulted on this section. For the whole of the three-miles distance between Rimrose Junction and Aintree the LOR trains had to be driven in "series" due to the main-line voltage being 630, against the 500 volts of the Overhead Railway. On the journey to Aintree the small LOR trains passed main-line special passenger trains, also goods trains hauled by steam locomotives, and seemed quite lost among the junctions and sidings encountered en-route. The race trains were always well patronised, not only by racegoers but also by railway enthusiasts who looked forward to making this rare journey every March. Starting on high embankments the trains continued past industrial plants such as the Bootle Tar Works, onwards through rock cuttings, under bridges, and past the vast acres of Aintree Sorting Sidings, different scenery indeed from that among which the trains spent most of their lives, amid dockland vistas.

To revert back to the Overhead Railway proper; the stations occurred in the following order travelling South to North: Dingle, Herculaneum, Toxteth, Brunswick, Wapping, Custom House, James Street, Pier Head, Princes, Clarence, Nelson, Huskisson, Canada, Brocklebank, Alexandra, Gladstone, Seaforth Sands, Seaforth & Litherland. All had the term Dock after their names except Dingle, Custom House, James Street, Pier head and the two Seaforth stations. In latter day practice "Dock" was omitted from new nameboards which replaced the metal signs when renewals became necessary, but only one or two stations actually received new nameboards. The "Dock" was not used on tickets either, so that a passenger could let his imagination play on a journey from Pier Head to Canada for instance! There was a station at Langton Dock from 1893 until 1906, and another at Sandon Dock also from 1893 until 1896. The former was closed, and the latter replaced by a new station at Nelson Dock. Custom House station was renamed Canning in 1945, as the wartime destruction of the building after which it was named rendered the title inappropriate. Canning was the name of the adjacent dock, and the area known as Canning Place was alongside the Custom House.

The chief station on the Liverpool Overhead Railway was the Pier Head edifice — an elaborate structure of timber and ironwork, and provided with platform awnings in addition to more commodious waiting rooms for the large numbers of passengers who used the premises. It was designed also to provide ample shelter from the chill wind that in Winter swept across the wide open area of the river frontage with nothing to break its force, and after the Royal Liver and Cunard Buildings had been erected roared through the canyon into which these structures had turned the lower end of Water Street. The shelter afforded by the timberwork of Pier Head station was certainly appreciated!

On the dock road section of the railway large BEWARE OF TRAINS notices warned passengers descending the stairways to look out for the steam locomotives that were continually at work hauling goods trains to and from the goods stations and quays, along the track which ran directly below the Overhead Railway structure. This track was crossed by intending passengers should they be proceeding to the platform furthest from their line of approach. Steam and smoke from the locomotives was diverted away from the girders of the LOR structure by means of a baffle-plate fitted to the engine's chimney, but this device was not fully effective so that over the years steam and heat took their toll, and assisted the elements in corroding the structure.

One of the less attractive features of the Liverpool Overhead Railway was the necessity of having to climb stairs in order to gain access to the station platforms, and the company were well aware that this was a drawback to elderly and infirm passengers. In 1901 a promising solution to this problem was tried out at Seaforth Sands in the shape of one of the first escalators to be employed at a railway station. This rather futuristic facility was known as the "Reno Inclined Elevator", and an LOR poster of the period depicted passengers of both sexes — men in top hats and frock coats (no workmen were shown!) and ladies attired a'la mode in long, elegantly styled dresses alighting from a tram and making their way up to the station platform by means of the new mechanical contrivance which was described as a "moving staircase". Unfortunately the "Reno", which was an inclined platform with rubber-covered ridges rather than an actual stairway-type escalator of the kind in use today, had a short and notorious existence. Although it performed its task satisfactorily, it had an unfortunate reputation for catching and tearing the lengthy skirts which were the mode of the time, and the company seem to have had a number of claims to meet in respect of ruined apparel. Little effort to overcome this difficulty appears to have been made, which was a pity because the escalator was a much appreciated amenity, and although successful machines of the kind were developed eventually, none were installed on the Liverpool Overhead Railway. A lift was thereafter provided at the new Seaforth Sands station of 1905, and this was used in peak hours to speed up the flow of passengers. As a matter of interest the first escalator to be installed on the London underground lines was at Earls Court station, in 1911, ten years after the Liverpool Overhead brought its experimental machine into operation.

The Overhead Railway bowstring girder bridge at James Street. A train passes above while tram No.184 prepares to pass beneath the structure on Saturday 28th June, 1954.

Photo J.W. Gahan.

Sunshine and shade at Pier Head station on a summer day in 1955. This was the busiest intermediate station on the railway and was provided with plenty of shelter.

Photo R.B. Parr.

A view from the platform of James Street station in August, 1955. The tram passing below is No.212. The last remnant of the "Goree" warehouses can be seen behind the trees.

Photo R.B. Parr.

A rebuilt train departing from Seaforth & Litherland station on a bleak day of snow in February, 1955. The presence of another train indicates dissarray of the schedule.

Photo N.N. Forbes.

Looking towards Seaforth from Seaforth Sands station. The train, terminating here will reverse direction via the crossover. This station was at the end of the actual "overhead", the track running onto an embankment beyond. August, 1955.

Photo J.A. Senior.

A tram pounds over the crossings with the M.D. & H.B. dockside railway while an "overhead" train passes above. A scene at the lower end of James Street, Liverpool in August, 1955.

Photo R.B. Parr.

A Liverpool Overhead train approaching Seaforth Sands station on its way to Dingle in June, 1956. Rimrose Road junction signal box is in the left middle background.

Photo R.B. Parr.

A train at Gladstone Dock station in 1956. The numbers on the open door of the driving compartment are those of the vehicles forming the three-carriage set.

Photo R. Stephens.

Onwards to Crosby — by Tram.

Early in the present century an "extension" to the Liverpool Overhead Railway was made from Seaforth Sands to Crosby. This was a conventional electric tramway on the streets built under Powers granted to the local councils of Waterloo-with-Seaforth, and Crosby, and leased to the railway company for 25 years. Construction of a tramway between Seaforth and Crosby had been talked about for many years, haulage by horses being visualised of course. A horse omnibus service was operated over the route by the Liverpool Corporation Tramways before the tramway was constructed, but was discontinued when electric trams commenced operation on 20th June, 1900. The system was of single track throughout, with numerous passing loops. The tram depot was situated at Seaforth Sands and was reached by a single line along a side street. The service, which proved to be popular and fulfilled a long-felt need was provided by a fleet of 16 tramcars, all except two being conventional double-deck open-top vehicles, but some had the upper decks closed-in eventually. The odd ones were single-deck cars of the popular Victorian "toast rack" type. All the cars were mounted on four-wheeled trucks of Brill design.

The trams were finished in a dignified livery of green and cream, in vivid contrast to the plain brown livery of the company's trains. The title LIVERPOOL OVERHEAD RAILWAY was lettered in full on the rocker panels of each tram, providing another puzzle for the stranger, that of finding a street tramway seemingly described as an overhead railway!

The tramway continued in operation until the company's lease ran out in 1925. Plans had been made for it to be taken over by the Liverpool Corporation and added to that body's already far-flung system of tramways, but a disagreement over fares put an end to the scheme and the last tram left Crosby for Seaforth Sands on the night of 31st December, 1925. Next day buses of the Waterloo & Crosby Motor Services Ltd., took over the former tram route, but in 1931 this company was merged into Ribble Motor Services Ltd., who still operate buses in the area. In its latter days the tramway became somewhat dilapidated, the effects of the late war not having been entirely overcome, and rail corrugation caused extremely noisy running of the cars. The single track with its passing loops did not make for satisfactory operation either, though had the Liverpool Corporation taken over as planned the line would doubtless have been doubled and the roads widened. All the trams were broken up at Seaforth Sands depot, and so ended an interesting offshoot of the "Overhead".

Very few relics of the Crosby tramway survived for long after its closure, but a short length of track lay embedded in the stone setts beneath the railway structure at Seaforth Sands station and actually survived the railway by about nine years, only being obliterated by road alterations in 1965. A large number of the standards that supported the overhead wires were retained for street lighting purposes until long after the second World War.

View from train rounding the curve on the approach to Herculaneum station after crossing the main line and yard of the Cheshire Lines Railway. 1956.

Photo J.B. Horne.

One of the modernised trains entering Seaforth Sands station in 1956.

Photo R. Stephens.

View from the platform of Huskisson Dock station in 1956. A Harrison Line ship is berthed at the quayside.

Photo J.A. Senior.

The Sights and Sounds of an Unforgettable Journey.

In order to appreciate the reason why the Liverpool Overhead was often referred to as the "Cosmopolitan Railway" it was necessary to ride the full length of the line. This was no ordinary train ride but an experience to remember, so let us therefore step back in time to the period immediately following the cessation of the Second World War and recall what a journey on the railway was really like before fading memory blanks out the experience for all time. It will be a nostalgic exercise to recall the sights and sounds as the train makes its way in retrospect from Dingle to Seaforth Sands above the streets that team with the traffic of World-wide sea trade. Probably more journeys to the far places of the Earth originated at stations on the LOR than on any railway in the land as hundreds of thousands of seafarers travelled on it to join their ships that lay alongside the line in the six miles of docks and quays along the Mersey shore. The Piccadilly Line of London Transport is the cosmopolitan railway of today as it serves the busy Heathrow Airport.

Having mentally put back the clock, we make our way to Dingle station, outside of which a poster is displayed with the eye-catching heading of "Compare these Fares", and upon studying the examples shown we find that, in general, travel on the Overhead Railway is less expensive than on the city's buses and trams. We obtain our tickets at the booking office just inside the cinema-like station entrance and proceed along the whitewashed passage through the subway and descend the stairs that lead down to the wide island platform. The electric lights seem dim after the sunshine outside but in a moment or two our eyes become accustomed to the artificial light and we can take stock of the scene. A couple of trains stand idly in the sidings awaiting the evening rush period to call them into traffic, but no service train is in at the moment. As we sit down on the platform seat we become accutely aware of the Victorian atmosphere that prevails, and would not be at all surprised to see a moustachioed gentlemen in a top hat and morning coat accompanied by a lady attired in the sweeping skirts of the "gay nineties" descending the stairs, the man indicating features of interest using a walking stick as a pointer and expounding on the wonders of electric traction! Such a couple would be entirely in keeping with the old-time atmosphere that clings to this improbable railway station. The dream is soon dispelled however by a distant rumbling in the tunnel that heralds the approach of a train. In a moment or two its headlight appears and it emerges from the gloom, hammering its way over the shining pattern of trackwork that reflects the station lights, and draws up at the platform, coming to a halt with a sigh of air brakes. The carriage doors are flung open and the detraining passengers make their way out of the station to the street above. Their places are soon taken by the waiting passengers, who enter the train and slam the doors unceremoniously behind them with a rattle of wooden-framed windows. After a moment or two the air-compressor bursts into life with its rhythmic tonk-tonk-tonk, ceasing when sufficient pressure has been built up in the brake reservoirs beneath the carriage floors. In the old days there were no compressors on the trains, a charge of air sufficient to last the journey out being obtained from an underground plant at each terminal station, or the carriage sheds.

In order to secure an undisturbed ride it is wise to choose a seat away from a door, and if scenic interest is the object of the journey, one on the riverward side of the train. The plain, buff-coloured and varnished brown interior of the carriage is gloomy beyond words after the brightness of the sunshine outside the station, and the passengers wait impatiently for the train to start its journey. On the platform the driver, holding the brass controller key which he carries from one end of the train to the other when reversing direction, is in deep conversation with the guard, who carries his inseparable red and green flags under his arm. Departure time at length arrives and the two men part company and take up their respective places in the train. After a brisk wave of the flag (the rebuilt trains have electric bells) the driver, upon observing that the signals are at green, notches round the handle mounted on top of the large controller and the train commences to roll, slamming and grunting as the wheels traverse the points and crossings prior to entering the tunnel for a run of half-a-mile or so in darkness, illuminated intermittently by blue flashes from the collector shoes on the live rail. The motor-hum and gear ringing are magnified in the confines of the tunnel. After a few moments all gloom is suddenly dispelled, bright sunshine banishing the darkness as the train runs out onto the high steel bridge that crosses the Cheshire Lines main line, sidings and the docks railway. As the train curves to run parallel with the River Mersey and line of docks, Brunswick locomotive depot can be seen on the Up side of the line, with rows of engines smoking quietly, awaiting their next turn of duty, whilst others are at work among the hundreds of goods wagons in the yards. On the Down side a splendid vista opens up — the broad River Mersey stretching away towards Garston, with the tall cranes of the ship-building yards visible on its opposite shore. Immediately below we see dockside quays, railway lines and roadways, and on the Up side a background of sheer rock face, elderly housing and industrial premises, also the gasholders along Grafton Street. The Dingle oil jetties are nearby the line and rows of oil storage tanks gleam in the sunlight, whilst lines of railway tank wagons and road tankers are prominent in the immediate vicinity.

A moment or two after leaving the bridge the train clatters over the junction that gives access to the carriage shed, which occupies the site of the original Herculaneum Dock station. It is a small corrugated iron structure at the end of a short spur, capable of holding two three-car trains. Ships mainly belonging to the Elder Dempster and Booker Lines are seen at rest in the docks, but rows of transit sheds hide the view of the river beyond. The train halts at the newer Herculaneum Dock station, at which a number of dock workmen enter, slamming the doors behind them, or leaving them open for the guard to close, after which, with a brisk wave of the green flag, he swings aboard quickly as the train starts. Once more on the move, for stops are brief, the train increases speed, motor gears humming and ringing and the carriage bodies twisting slightly as the train encounters undulations in the bridge structure as it follows the levels of the dock road. Note now the two-aspect colour-light signals which are of such brilliance that they are visible from a distance of 3,000 feet, even in bright sunshine, their installation being the first of its kind in Britain and has been in use since it replaced an automatic semaphore system in 1921. There are only two regularly manned signal boxes on the railway nowadays, at Dingle and Seaforth Sands, where shunting operations need to be carried out. Signal boxes are situated also at Herculaneum Dock, for the carriage shed, and at Alexandra Dock, the latter two being opened as required. The mechanical semaphore system has been retained at each terminus where reversals and other manoeuvres are necessary, also at Herculaneum which has both semaphore and light signals. Emergency crossovers are provided at several intermediate stations, being operated by lever frames on the station platforms. These crossovers were of great value during the late war when sections of the railway were put out of action through bomb damage and short-workings had to be instituted. The colour-light system includes a train-stopping device that applies the brakes should a train overshoot a stop signal. The trains signal themselves as they proceed, altering the signal aspects behind them and maintaining a safety margin between each train on the intensive service. The railway has been worked without a single serious operating mishap since it was opened far back in 1893.

The train is now approaching Toxteth Dock station, the dock itself being occupied mainly by Elder Dempster and Moss Hutchinson ships. To the right looms the immense red-brick Brunswick goods warehouse of the Cheshire Lines Railway, whilst on the riverward side there are rows of dock sheds and other buildings, with parallel railway tracks that throw off branches to the various quays. As the train proceeds on its way the bomb-shattered ruins of the South Docks goods station of the London, Midland & Scottish Railway (formerly L & NW and L & Y) are seen on the landward side of the line. These weed-covered reminders of the grim days and turbulent nights of 1940 and 1941 are long abandoned, their rails and turntables buried under rubble, or removed altogether, and their bricks and ironwork toppled to the ground. It is now difficult to picture in the mind the once busy premises that were burned or blasted into shattered wastes, never to re-open. Such scenes of blitzed warehouses and other buildings were common along the entire length of the dock road, but rebuilding projects are already beginning to obliterate these reminders of more stirring times, and such relics will disappear completely in the course of time. One cannot ride on the Overhead Railway however, without recalling the scenes of chaos and destruction all along the docks, the fallen masonry, charred beams and twisted girders of all kinds of buildings, wrecked railway and road vehicles, also sunken ships that were part and parcel of the Liverpool scene when the city and docks were in the front line of the Battle of the Atlantic. Indeed, on many occasions the Overhead Railway itself was badly damaged and complete spans blasted off their columns, notably at Wapping, James Street and Canada Dock. James Street station was totally destroyed and had to be completely rebuilt. Between this station and Pier Head a bomb blasted tons of stonework onto the structure from the Mersey Tunnel ventilating shaft. On more than one occasion great fires raged a few yards from the railway, such as on the night that the Wapping warehouses were ignited and a great deal of wreckage crashed down onto the structure. How the railway survived seems a mircale, but the company and its staff were resourceful and energetic, and all hands turned to the task of clearing up while engineers carried out urgent repairs after every "incident" as such interuptions to normal life and business were termed in the war years. The trials and problems were enormous, but they were overcome and normal train services resumed as quickly as possible. The gaps in the railway were temporarily filled by hired buses which shuttled to and fro linking the sections still workable.

The company's head office in James Street was completely destroyed during the air raids, and after several temporary abodes, including in a train at Seaforth Sands, refuge was found in Hargreaves Building in Chapel Street. By great good fortune the workshops were not badly damaged, as a direct hit here would have proved disastrous as no replacement rolling stock was available to substitute for the specially built trains — no main-line trains would have been suitable for use on the system owing to severe weight restrictions.

The Overhead Railway, along with the city's trams provided adequate transport during the war, at a time when motor bus services had to be curtailed and closed down in mid-evening owing to fuel problems. The trains and trams used home-produced fuel, and were thus independent of fuel oil and petrol, commodities that had to be brought from overseas countries at great risk due to the submarine menace, and the continual risk of attack by hostile aircraft. By contrast, the coal that was the source of power for the tramways and local electric railways came from South Lancashire or Yorkshire, involving transport only over short distances.

While we have been reflecting upon past glories the train has arrived at Brunswick Dock station, and our gaze alights on more Elder Dempster ships and vessels of the Harrison Line, together with smaller cargo ships including those of the Isle of Man Steam Packet Company. Narrow streets of warehouses, dwellings and various kinds of industrial premises fill the scene on the landward side of the railway, with the tall modern tenement blocks of Caryl Street on higher ground nearby.

After leaving Brunswick the train passes along fairly rapidly, the wheels beating out their tireless rythm on the short rail lengths. Liverpool Cathedral now swims into view, its great brown sandstone form towering majestically above St. James's Mount and dominating a vast area of buildings, many of them very old and in a state of dilapidation. On the riverward side is Queens Dock with its branches, followed by Kings Dock, with ships of the Booth Line and Palm Line alongside their quays. The vast white concrete building on the left is a modern grain silo, built in 1936, which stands near to an equally vast but older brick silo. Several floating grain elevators in the dock alongside transfer grain from ship to silo. At intervals as we proceed the muffled sound of a tolling bell and a cloud of steam billowing out from beneath the LOR structure indicates the presence of a dock steam locomotive making its way along the road with a rake of goods wagons. The double track of the docks railway runs directly below the LOR structure for most of its length and numerous branches lead to goods stations and wharves. The large railway warehouse on the left as the train enters Wapping station is that known as Park Lane Goods, the first rail depot on the dock estate, built by the Liverpool & Manchester Railway long ago in the year 1830, and enlarged greatly by the London & North Western system. There were few docks when this patriarch of goods stations was built however — the great expansion was yet to come, hastened by the development of railways, also the introduction of steam propulsion at sea, which permitted ever-larger ships to be built.

A little further along Wapping stand, side by side, the Wapping and Salthouse goods stations, built by the Lancashire & Yorkshire Railway Company to enable them to share in the South Docks goods traffic, and these are reached over the dock lines. We might catch sight here of one of the tiny "Pug" Saddle Tank engines that work the dock road traffic between these depots and the North Docks. Just beyond the goods stations is Canning Place, and a desolate waste of rubble-strewn land. Here stood the great Custom House, a huge, impressive domed building which was opened in 1831, and was one of Liverpool's most notable architectural classics. It was damaged in one of the earliest air attacks, in the late Summer of 1940 and totally destroyed in a later raid, the remains being subsequently demolished. The basement was turned into a huge emergency water reservoir for fire fighting purposes for the remainder of the war. Custom House station, which was situated immediately opposite the old building was renamed Canning in 1945 as the original title had no relevance after Customs activities had, perforce, been transferred elsewhere. Approaching this station the vast Wapping warehouse dating from the 1850's, extensively damaged in the war and since repaired, looms high above the railway, cutting off all sight of the docks, whilst along the dock road on the landward side, ships chandlers, sail-makers, ships stores suppliers, small workshops and so on are mingled with public houses, tobacconists, cocoa rooms and snack bars that line the roadway. Ancient gas lamps contrast with the brilliant electric signals of the railway above them, and along the highway and its narrow tributaries flows the ceaseless commercial traffic of the busy port.

As the train proceeds, the passengers on the landward side will not see ships, but are granted fleeting glimpses of the other side of dockland life. Behind glass windows large and small, one sees clerks at their desks in the mostly old and gloomy offices, girls in blue overalls at benches in a clothing manufacturer's premises, men queueing up at lunch time in the cocoa rooms for pint mugs of tea and inch-thick sandwiches! In the pubs groups of men converse or argue at the bar, while others congregate on the pavement outside, or on an open piece of land on which once stood a building. Groups of seafaring men, including those bands of Coolies who walk along in single-file, mingle with the men of Merseyside in the cosmopolitan port. Traffic, from large horse-drawn drays to steam wagons convey goods between the warehouses and docks. Occasionally a steam traction engine is seen hauling a boiler or some other outsize load but these machines are very rare nowadays. Numbers of traction engines, including agricultural and fairground types found a new task allotted to them during the blitz — that of pulling down the tottering walls of damaged buildings and some of these engines lay abandoned in dockland streets after completion of the clearing-up operations. Curiously, a showman's engine named "Queen Elizabeth" lay for many months in Juniper Street, Bootle, still in its gay showground colours, its resting place amid tall warehouses being the very antithesis of the crowded fairground. (At the time few people paid any attention to such machines, but those that survive in the 1980's are rare and very valuable treasures that have been expensively and painstakingly restored as museum pieces.)

Salthouse Dock, now on our left, cannot be seen clearly owing to the roofs of transit sheds cutting off the view from the train, but Albert Dock with its colonaded warehouses is glimpsed, as it lies further off towards the river. This dock is a lasting monument to Jesse Hartley, the Engineer of the Liverpool docks for many years, who designed this dock and warehouses as a single complex. They are

50

now ancient, having been opened far back in the year 1845. Another ancient warehouse nearby is the Dukes, which was built in 1811 as a barge terminal for vessels of the Bridgewater Canal. These vessels could sail right inside through the great arches in the warehouse walls, to load or discharge cargo under cover.

Canning Dock alongside the railway is a venue for small vessels and cargo ships, mainly those sailing to and from Ireland. This picturesque old dock with its quiet waters and ancient quays, with a vista of the Pier Head buildings in the background forms a scene which is popular with Merseyside artists and has often been portrayed on canvas. Here grab cranes are busy unloading sand from small vessels with tall black funnels. The sand dredged from the river bed, is used for building purposes. At Canning Dock too, one sometimes meets retired seafarers sitting on bollards smoking their pipes and always ready to chat about the joys and hardships of life at sea.

The train is now approaching the commercial centre of the city and pulls up in James Street station, which is a busy one, for here passengers change from train to tram, bus or ferry (or vice versa). This station serves many commercial buildings — the shipping and insurance offices which are extemely numerous in this quarter. Only a few-hundred yards away is the James Street station of the underground Mersey Railway, which handles vast numbers of passengers travelling between Liverpool and Birkenhead. So here we have railways on three levels — the Overhead, docks railway for goods traffic at street level, and the Mersey Railway deep below the surface.

Immediately beyond James Street the line curves slightly North-Westward crossing the street on an imposing bowstring-girder bridge after which the line curves North again to pass right against the Mersey road tunnel ventilating shaft and close-by the Dock Board, Cunard and Royal Liver Buildings, the great Liverpool waterfront trio which form a skyline known throughout the World. Brunswick Street and Water Street, both busy approach roads to the Pier Head are crossed by normal spans, and on the North side of the last-named thoroughfare, Pier Head station is situated. On the curved sections of line just mentioned, devices known as flange lubricators are provided on the rails to minimise friction and noise. There is little "wheel squeal" here, only a gentle whine as the flanges bear on the rail-heads. A film of grease, which the wheels receive as they pass over the lubricator is spread along the inner edge of the rail by their passage and is extremely effective in reducing noise and bite.

As the train draws into Pier Head station we see, on the landward side the blitzed remains of the ancient colonaded warehouses known as the Goree Piazzas, erected as long ago as 1803 and heavily damaged by bombs during the war. The buildings were named after the island of Goree which is off the West coast of Africa, and formed a large and tangible link with the old sailing ship days. They imparted a touch of old Spain to the area, with their colonades of shady arches behind which were stores concerned with ships supplies and eating places. After dark the colonades became the haunt of destitutes and the "shady ladies" of the dockland scene. So high were these warehouses that, in conjunction with the three famed Pier Head buildings they formed a canyon which was in shadow for most of the day, through which the busy dock road and rail traffic continually streamed. To our left, the Royal Liver Building with its high, twin clock towers, each crowned by an enormous effigy of the mythical Liver Bird, rears upwards to a height of 300 feet above the roadway. The building occupies land that was formerly water — Georges Dock which was filled-in to make a solid river frontage in the early years of the present century. The dock was still in use for small shipping when the Overhead Railway was built, and when one went to the Pier Head in a horse-drawn tram, one gazed upon the decks of sailing ships as the car crossed the swing bridge that spanned the passage between George's and Canning Docks.

At Pier Head station many passengers alight from, and others join the train, for this is the busiest station on the railway, serving as it does the commercial district of the city, in addition to connecting with many tram and bus routes, and also the cross-river ferries that arrive and depart day and night at the nearby George's Landing Stage. The ocean liners berth at the North end, known as the Princes Landing Stage, as it is adjacent to the dock of that name. Vessels for the Isle of Man and Llandudno also use the landing stages here. Alas, ocean liners serve Liverpool to a decreasing extent, as Southampton long ago became a more convenient terminal, but air travel threatens to render the passenger liner obsolete. In time only cargo shipping is likely to be seen in the Mersey, so long host to the great passenger vessels. It will be a sad day when the last of them sails out from the Mersey, but that time is not just yet however. The more gracious and leisurely mode of trans-ocean travel which is their hallmark will eventually be recalled with acute nostalgia in Liverpool.

Almost every train picks up or sets down dock workers at the Pier Head station, and strangers to the city are apt to be puzzled by the salutations as the men greet each other cheerily — the Liverpool vernacular is little understood by non-residents. There is none of the reserve which characterises passengers on the main-line railways, and conversation is carried on loudly and freely for all to hear. "Ullo whack", or "whereareyerwerkinlads" are two Liverpudlianisms one may hear. The men settle on their seats and open up newspapers, many beginning with the back page, whilst pipes and cigarettes are ignited with matches struck on the floor, on the window glass or the sole of a boot. Shop talk is carried on vociferously and continues unabated as the men travel between the various docks. On Mondays mornings discussion chiefly centres on the previous Saturday's football matches with scathing witticisms directed at each other by rival Everton and Liverpool supporters. Yes indeed, travel on the Overhead Railway is an education in many things!

Immediately after pulling away from the Pier Head, the train crosses another bowstring-girder bridge and passes above the wide, busy approach to the River frontage. On the landward side the weathered tower of St. Nicholas church, crowned by a gilt figure of a sailing ship presents an improbable picture in this commercial landscape, though the church was here long before any docks were built! The war-damaged nave of the old church is at present a weed-covered ruin having been destroyed in the air raids of the late war. This hallowed place of worship with its pleasant gardens forms a quiet haven of peace and tranquility amid intense traffic and activity, though once upon a time its sandstone walls were washed by the Mersey at times of extra high tides, before the land was made-up and docks built. Today the church is flanked by the white marble Tower Building on its South side and Chapel Street on its North side. The concrete portal of the Mersey Road tunnel (Docks Branch) forms a dramatic contrast between old and new on the North side of Chapel Street. The tunnel, burrowing beneath the quaintly named narrow warehouse-lined street of Lancelots Hey persues a curving course to join the main tunnel that, running parallel with the Mersey Railway tunnel, lies far below the track level of the Overhead Railway.

Suddenly the dock road commences again, rather narrow and lined by very old warehouses on the landward side for some distance North of the Pier Head, but before entering this section the train crosses a second bowstring-girder bridge and perhaps one of the city's trams will pass beneath at the same time, providing additional interest. In this area three double-track street tramways cross the docks railway beneath the Overhead line. Speaking of trams reminds us that the Overhead Railway was built some years before the city tramways were electrified, so that horse-drawn trams and omnibuses passed beneath the structure, again presenting a vivid contrast between old and new in an earlier period of transport development.

The stretch of dock road below is named New Quay, and shortly after becomes Bath Street, followed by Waterloo Road — all the one continuous roadway, which finally becomes Regent Road. To the left lies Princes Dock, used mostly by ships to and from Belfast and Dublin. The view of the dock is however, cut off by a lengthy transit shed. On the road within the dock walls are hordes of lorries and vans, railway wagons and stacks of cargo awaiting shipment. Soon the immense Bibby's seed mills appear on the right, and also the railway crossing on Waterloo Road that allows mainline passenger trains to reach the Riverside station. Our train is now travelling quite fast, rocking slightly as it negotiates the gentle curves as the railway follows the line of the dock road, and runs non-stop through Princes Dock station, now closed. Towering above us on the riverward side are the enormous twin Waterloo grain warehouses, built in 1867, with lorries and railway wagons being loaded alongside. To the right is the large and extensive Waterloo Dock goods station, the first part of which was opened by the London & North Western Railway in 1849, and extended as traffic increased. On the left now lie Victoria and Trafalgar Docks, havens of smaller ships, followed by Clarence Dock, though only the graving dock remains, the large "wet" dock having been filled-in and an electric power station built on the site in 1931. This establishment looms high above the train and we look with interest at the mountain of coal stacked in an extensive well for the ever-hungry furnaces, and the busy steam locomotives ceaselessly shunting loaded steel hopper wagons into the station and bringing out the empties, their wheel flanges emitting piercing shrieks as they traverse the sharply curved grooved rails laid in concrete. The plain tubular concrete chimneys at this power station are appropriately known as the "Ugly Sisters".

Clarence Dock station is next reached, beyond which, on the landward side of the railway stands the colossus of the docks — the Stanley Tobacco Warehouse, an immense edifice 14 storeys high and which swallowed up 27,000,000 bricks in its construction. Built in 1900, it is nevertheless still one of the largest warehouses in the World, and strangers gaze at it in awe as the train passes close-by. In one corner of the warehouse yard is a small brick building with a tall chimney, containing a furnace, the purpose of which is to destroy sub-standard weed, the fragrance of which drifts on the wind and brings forth exclamations of disgust from some of the dock workmen whom would, no doubt, be willing to perform the burning operation free of charge in their own miniature furnaces! This destructor is known as the "Kings Pipe".

Immediately after passing the tobacco warehouse we reach Stanley Dock, which is linked with the nearby Leeds & Liverpool Canal by a flight of five locks. The entrance to this dock, the only one on the landward side of the Overhead Railway, is crossed by the previously-mentioned combined swing and lifting bridge, and on passing over this novel structure the carriage wheels clump heavily as they encounter the joints between movable and fixed bridgework. Here passengers can look directly down into the water and is the only location where this can be done, as the railway does not cross any other waterway. Nowadays Stanley Dock is used only by small vessels, so that it is seldom that the bridge needs to be swung open, though the lower lifting portion has to be operated to allow ships into and out of the dock on frequent occasions.

Collingwood and Salisbury Docks are next passed in quick

succession. These docks are frequented by fairly small vessels, among users being the Clyde Shipping Company, Irish & Mersey Line etc. A landmark of captivating interest can be seen on the left, near the river, in the form of an extraordinary six-sided tower with a clock on each — a fortress-like edifice which was designed by Jesse Hartley and built in 1848. Resembling something from a fairy tale, the old tower has stood guard on its quayside through decade after decade of wind, weather and wars, and with its immensely solid construction could probably last for centuries.

On proceeding further through the heart of dockland the vast and impressive variety of shipping is displayed for the interested gaze of everyone, and the names of shipping companies spelt out in large characters on dock sheds and walls are familiar throughout the oceans. We read them as we pass — Cunard, Ellerman, Pacific Steam Navigation, Brocklebank, Blue Star, Blue Funnel, Lykes Lines. These are just a small selection from many more. The variety of inward-and outward-bound cargoes on the quaysides is such as to give rise to absolute astonishment. Here lie sections of tree trunks several feet in diameter from far-distant forests, stacks and stacks of cut timber, crated machinery, railway carriages and wagons, motor cars, vans, tractors, lorries, army vehicles and tanks in desert camouflage. Also iron pipes, bales of cotton and a host of other items which the tall cranes whisk into or out of the deep holds of cargo ships. The activity too, is intense, and at each urgent station stop passengers board or alight from the trains in considerable numbers. If one takes stock of fellow travellers the fact emerges that they are mostly men — woman passengers are much in the minority in the middle of the day, but they are fairly numerous at weekends or holiday times when the trains are filled with sight-seers. Not only does the passenger complement consist of local men, but scores of seafarers, many of them members of the coloured races ride the trains between the various docks and the beckoning city. The station staff have a difficult time interpreting the many questions put before them, especially those from persons with little or no understanding of English, but their experience stands them in good stead in this respect in having developed a kind of instinct for comprehending the queries and giving the right answers, sometimes in sign language! The passengers converse in a variety of tongues and the atmosphere inside the carriage becomes heavy with the fug and aroma of a considerable range of tobacco's from pipes, cigarettes or cigars. To enjoy riding on the "Overhead" one must appreciate the spirit and mystique of all this.

Travelling onwards, there are more and yet more docks, warehouses, railway yards and engineering workshops, many of the last-named being concerned with repairs to ship components. Our small train rumbles along, passing every few minutes one proceeding in the opposite direction with a rush and a rattle. After Nelson Dock station the Bramley-Moore switchback section is the next item of interest so far as the Overhead Railway is concerned. Here the line descends to street level in order to pass beneath the high-level railway that serves the coal tips, and this section is taken at a fair speed, the rumbling sound of the bridgework being replaced by the more familiar muffled roar of ballasted track. We catch here a glimpse of a wagon-load of coal being tipped into the hold of a grimy tall-funnelled steamer bound for Dublin or elsewhere, a great cloud of black dust drifting away on the wind as the grubby contents of the wagon fall in an avalanch — 12 tons at a time. Lines of loaded coal wagons await their turn on the elevated coal tip tracks, shunted to and from the dock by the sturdy old L & Y "Pug" Saddle Tank engines that do so much of the dock work in Liverpool, along with MD & HB engines.

Shortly after the train has regained the bridge structure the passenger looking out on the riverward side will notice a strange gap in the otherwise continuous line of docks, and may wonder why this should be so. The explanation lays in the fact that the site, which is now occupied by huts, small sheds and cargo, was once the Huskisson No.2 Dock which was wiped off the surface of the earth on the Sunday morning of 4th May, 1941 when the steamer "Malakand" loaded with munitions was ignited by a burning dockside shed, and despite heroic work by firemen and crew in an effort to subdue the blaze and save the ship, exploded with devastating results. Naturally, the adjacent Overhead Railway structure was extensively damaged, the dockside sheads were reduced to rubble and so was the dock in which the ship was berthed, and all that remained of the vessel was a twisted mass of mangled steel in the muddy water. The dock, being so heavilty damaged, was filled-in. This was only one of many incidents on that morning of drama in the period of the blitz when the Overhead Railway was in the front line of battle and exposed to constant peril.

The train is now approaching the docks used by the largest ships including ocean-going passenger liners, and we are treated to splendid views of vessels, the massive hulls of which tower above the railway. Ships are to be seen in both wet docks and dry (graving) docks. In the latter they stand high and dry, the full depth of their great hulls being clearly visible whilst men work around them on staging. Painters are seen at work, sitting in cradles slung over the sides of the vessels and appear tiny in comparison with the monsters to which they give their attention. Tall cranes atop transit sheds swing cargo aboard ships moored at the quaysides and a constant procession of lorries and goods trains passes along the dock road. The fascinating scene from the Overhead Railway is apt to implant seeds of discontent in the minds of many city workers — an urge to travel and see the great wide world outside! Many a passenger whose days are spent in a shop or office envies the men who sail in these ships to the far places of the Earth, away from the routine of town life, to warmer, sunnier places. Regular passengers know most, if not all the colours of the funnels and house flags of the British shipping companies and a good many foreign ones too. Discussions on ships are commonplace in the trains among the sailors and dock workers, some of whom will explain the sights and sounds to strangers making their first trip on the railway. They emphasise the fact that there is no comparable train ride anywhere in the World, and they are quite right of course!

Brocklebank, Canada and Langton Docks are passed successively, then Alexandra Dock with its cold storage depot. Ships and cranes still dominate the riverward side — engineering works, warehouses and railway yards fill the scene on the landward side. After passing Brocklebank Dock, the train negotiates a severe curve and the railway parts company with the main dock road which continues straight ahead, so that railway sidings intervene between the road and dock walls. Below, on the right-hand side lies the extensive North Mersey goods yard and the fortress-like buildings of the Alexandra Granary adjacent to Strand Road. The docks which we have passed in the last few minutes are used mainly by ships of the Ellerman, Furness Withy, Blue Star and Blue Funnel Lines.

The next station reached is that serving Gladstone Dock. The graving dock was opened as long ago as 1913, but the wet wet docks and further graving docks of the Gladstone system were built as recently as 1927. This area is the haunt of the great Cunard and Canadian Pacific ships, not forgetting the late, lamented White Star Line (now merged with Cunard) whose popular ships once graced these docks. When such a celebrity among ships as the old "Mauritania" of the Cunard Line visited Gladstone Dock she proved a magnet that attracted many extra passengers to the Overhead Railway, from the trains of which a perfect and extensive view of the great ship was presented. At Gladstone ships of the United States Line, Blue Funnel Line and New Zealand Shipping Company will also be noted. The variety of cargo ships from all parts of the World present a scene to be remembered in its colourful variety.

Gladstone Dock station has two footbridges over the railway and here witty passengers delight in telling us that they can walk over the "Overhead". The station was opened in 1930 and the bridges were required because the Up platform is within the walls of the North Mersey goods yard, so that all passengers must leave the premises via the Down platform. A footbridge was also provided at Huskisson for a similar reason. It is not possible to enter the dock estate without a permit nowadays, and mention of this necessary document brings to mind the fact that in days before the 1939-45 war an excellent facility offered by the LOR was the issue, with a Round Trip ticket, of a permit to visit ocean liners in the docks. This extremely popular facility was not restored after the war, but the Round Trip tickets, which were very good value for a modest fare were re-introduced and were much in demand by visitors to Liverpool. The Liner permits, needless to say, were eagerly obtained as they gave the holder the opportunity of inspecting at close quarters an ocean ship, on which the chances were that he or she would never have the pleasure of making a voyage.

Having passed Gladstone Dock and hardly digested this final show of the port's greatness, we find ourselves nearing journey's end, as we are not travelling onwards to Seaforth & Litherland. Not every train goes the whole way — some turn back at Seaforth Sands. Now, with the wheel flanges biting hard at the rails, the train is swinging slowly round the curve, passing above the main dock highway again (here named Shore Road), and after clattering across the points and crossings of the most complex trackwork on the line, draws up in Seaforth Sands station. On the last few-hundred yards the docks give way to a vista of yellow sands stretching away Northwards to Crosby and Southport, New Brighton with its lighthouse and old fort, and ships in the Mersey estuary with long wraiths of smoke trailing from their funnels. It is a very pleasant picture and a fitting climax to an unforgettable journey.

The scenery on the final stretch of the line between Seaforth Sands and Seaforth & Litherland stations is mixed — old and new housing, factories, shops and so on, with grass and wild plants on the slopes of the embankment bringing touches of colour to an otherwise rather drab area. The skyline is fascinatingly varied however, despite the blitz of the war years having removed quite a few buildings which were once prominent features of the landscape.

Many passengers, including holders of Round Trip tickets alight from the train at Seaforth Sands and make their way out of the station by descending the long, narrow stairway into the street, the "Round-Trippers" ascending the stairway on the opposite side of the line for the return journey. Taking stock of our surroundings, we note the LOR workshops on the opposite side of Fort Road, and the main road to Crosby along which the company's trams once ran, and we examine the short length of remaining tramway track still in the stone setts beneath the railway structure. Walking round the corner under the railway bridge we see the polished, busy rails of the Liverpool Corporation Tramways, with a couple of trams and buses at the terminus adjacent to the station, whilst the red buses of the Ribble company pass to and fro, some of them serving the district once traversed by the "Overhead" trams. All is hurry and bustle about the station area and a fresh breeze blows in from the open sea. The ships and cranes of Gladstone Dock in the near background merit a short walk along Fort Road in order to get a closer look. Seaforth Sands was once a popular resort for people of Bootle and Liverpool, as it had a strip of beach noted for quicksands, so one did not bathe or paddle, but stayed close to the landward edge of the beach. New works carried out in more recent times obliterated the old footpath that led to the shore. A large area of land North of Seaforth Sands station, once part of the estate of Seaforth Hall, built in 1840 by J. Muspratt, the chemicals magnate, is occupied by sidings, the MD & HB Engineer's depot, and stacks of imported timber.

For the sake of the experience, we will travel back to Liverpool in the evening rush period which begins to get into its hectic stride at about half-past four. We will find the experience another one to remember, and will forcibly realise why it was necessary to build the railway in the first place. The train service is considerably increased by extras, which are now emerging from the sheds and sidings to join in the task of getting the dock workers home. The carriages become tightly packed with home-going overalled men in peaked caps or battered trilby's until there is scarcely room to breath, and at each station along the line the platforms are thronged with prospective passengers up to six-deep. As soon as the train comes to a halt the doors are flung open and they pile in, and woe betide anyone trying to alight! Courtesy is an absent virtue but everyone is cheerful and much banter is exchanged between various groups of men. The Liverpool dockers are past masters at quickly boarding crowded trains and having to stand does not worry them as long as they are on the way home with the minimum of delay. Sometimes several will commence to sing and others will join-in until the atmosphere becomes positively sociable, with an occasional good humoured admonition to "shut up" from colleagues trying to read their copies of the Liverpool Echo. The open type carriages are just right for conviviality, and occasionally a dockland evangelist is encountered, taking the opportunity of getting in some salvation work as the train rumbles along, with a conspicious lack of success! The "No Smoking" notices displayed in some carriages are considered to be purely ornamental, and the air is heavy with haze from numerous pipes and cigarettes puffed at full blast.

The majority of the passengers alight at the Pier Head station, at which the staff have a busy time closing carriage doors and collecting tickets as train after train arrives and disgorges its hordes of homewardbound workers. With cheery "good-nights" and that famous Liverpool parting shot "Tarrah" the men file down the stairs to join tram and bus queues for the next stage of their journeys. Here too, we take our leave of the railway and retire to a seat by the landing stage to discuss a few remaining points about the "Dockers Umbrella" which we have seen in action today.

Apart from the overwhelming fascination of the dockland scene, a journey on the Liverpool Overhead Railway proved an education in other aspects — it was a geography and history lesson combined.

Most visitors naturally looked at the docks and ships, but the scene on the landward side of the line was also full of interest for those who cared to look. Regular travellers soon learned by heart the names of the many streets that lead down to the waterfront, as well as the names and origins of the many railway depots, engineering works, warehouses and so on. An "Overhead" train commenced its journey either end of the line in what are the "newer" districts, although by the time of this description they present an old and weatherbeaten look which the blitz furthered. Few, if any, of the buildings at the Seaforth or Dingle extremities of the line are much more than a century old, but the really ancient (and partly most modernised) district is passed through near the centre of Liverpool. Here was originally situated the small, quiet fishing village on the creek of the Mersey that was known as "The Pool" — an inlet which was converted into the first dock far back in 1715, and which became the nucleus of the future great seaport and city. The area eventually became known as "Sailor Town" and something of the old atmosphere still lingers in the vicinity of Canning and Salthouse Docks. It became a shady district of taverns and various unsavoury premises, with narrow streets, courts of slum dwellings mixed with warehouses and the stores of ships suppliers. Although most of this vanished, for the dwellings and ale houses were later replaced by shops and industrial premises in the late nineteenth century, the old cobbled quays and warehouses remain much as they were in the days of sailing ships. The advanced age of many warehouse buildings and many of the industrial premises, plus their increasing unsuitability for latter day business means that their days are inevitably numbered and a new look is already becoming apparent as old dockside transit sheds are replaced by new ones, whilst other buildings are rising on the sites of old ones which were destroyed in the wartime bombing. Although the whole area traversed by the Overhead Railway is one of industry and commerce, the discerning eye can rest on a scene that possesses its own particular kind of beauty. There is little greenery to be seen apart from weeds however, as the last tree vanished long ago from Liverpool's dockland, once an area of fields leading down to yellow sands, something hard to imagine today. At night the scene becomes one of myriads of tiny lights from the portholes of innumerable ships, the glow of their deck lights and navigation lamps. The gas lamps along the dock road shed their mellow pools of radiance on the paving stones, whilst the brilliant red and green signal lights on the Overhead Railway add intense splashes of colour to the picture. Sometimes late at night a train is the only sign of life along the docks except for the policemen keeping watch from their little gatehouses, sailors returning to ships or occasional night shift men going to work.

The docks are not always a hive of frantic activity as they were seven days a week during the war. There are quiet times, such as

Saturday afternoons, Sundays and Bank Holidays when work slackens off, though even at the quietest periods there are men at work somewhere along the docks. The Overhead Railway maintains a frequent service on these days but tourists largely replace the dock workers. There is still plenty to see, though cranes are still, shunting engines in their sheds and rows of railway wagons stand idle in the sunshine. Walking along the road below the railway structure at such times, the sound of an approaching train can be discerned by a faint rumbling, increasing in intensity until, with a pounding of wheels on the rail joints it passes directly overhead, with motors humming and gears ringing, then gradually fades into the distance and silence reigns once more, except for a passing motor vehicle, the screaming of gulls or the occasional siren call by a ship in the river.

So much was the Overhead Railway embedded into the consciousness of Liverpool's population that threats to its continued existence hardly made any impression, but the railway's traffic was affected from time to time. The horse-drawn omnibuses of early days offered little competition, but the coming of the electric trams posed a crisis of no small order. This was overcome, as we have already noted, by speeding up the trains. Trade depression hit the revenue on several occasions, and so did travelling habits on the part of the public. Perhaps the strangest competitor however was the telephone, the general introduction of which drastically reduced the numbers of dockland messengers who were extensive users of the railway when messages had to be delivered by hand. Mechanisation at the docks and the reduced crew complements of steamships, and later still motor ships as compared with the old sailing ships also took their toll of traffic.

The junction at Herculaneum Dock, showing the small carriage shed on the site of the original terminus (before the Dingle extension was built). Photographed on a dull December day in 1956.

Photo J. Maher.

A Sunday scene in December, 1956. A Dingle-bound train near Huskisson Dock. In the background stands the enormous Midland Railway Sandon Goods warehouse.

Photo J. Maher.

A view of Fort Road, showing Seaforth Sands station on the left-hand side, and the L.O.R. carriage shed and workshops on the right. July, 1957.

Photo J. Maher.

The girder bridge and tunnel portal at Herculaneum Dock, July, 1957 (after closure of the L.O. Railway).

Photo N.N. Forbes.

A modernised train at Seaforth Sands with a crowd of passengers waiting to board. A late 1956 scene.

Photo J.A. Senior.

Huskisson Dock station photographed from a footbridge "over the overhead" in December, 1956.

Photo J. Maher.

An "overhead" train passing Seaforth South signal box and about to traverse the crossover to bring it to the platform of Seaforth & Litherland station.
Photo: J.A. Senior.

"Grand National" Saturday, March 1948. A race-day special train from Dingle to Aintree crosses from the L.O.R. to the ex L & Y North Mersey Branch at Rimrose Road Junction.

Photo N.N. Forbes.

"Grand National" day, 1956. A special train bound for Aintree passes another train at James Street station.

Photo R. Stephens.

GRAND NATIONAL

SATURDAY, 26th, MARCH, 1955.

TRAVEL BY

OVERHEAD RAILWAY

WITHOUT CHANGING

DIRECT TO AINTREE RACECOURSE

		a.m.	a.m.	p.m.	p.m.	p.m.	p.m.	p.m.	p.m.	p.m.
DINGLE	dep.	11 25	11 40	12 25	12 35	1 5	1 14	1 23	1 37	1 54
JAMES STREET	,,	11 35	11 50	12 35	12 45	1 15	1 24	1 33	1 47	2 4
PIER HEAD	,,	11 37	11 52	12 37	12 47	1 17	1 26	1 35	1 49	2 6
SEAFORTH SANDS	,,	11 53	12 8	12 53	1 3	1 33	1 42	1 53	2 9	2 23
AINTREE (No. 3 Platform)	arr.	12 2	12 16	1 1	1 13	1 41	1 52	2 3	2 18	2 32

		p.m.	p.m.	p.m.	p.m.	p.m.	p.m.	p.m.
AINTREE	dep.	3 50	4 7	4 24	4 42	4 51	5 1	5 31
SEAFORTH SANDS	,,	4 4	4 19	4 31	4 51	5 4	5 12	5 41
PIER HEAD	,,	4 18	4 33	4 48	5 5	5 18	5 26	5 55
JAMES STREET	,,	4 19	4 34	4 49	5 6	5 19	5 27	5 56
DINGLE	arr.	4 28	4 43	4 53	5 15	5 28	5 36	6 5

FARES from	Single	Return
DINGLE, HERCULANEUM, TOXTETH, BRUNSWICK, WAPPING and CANNING	1/-	2/-
JAMES STREET PIER HEAD CLARENCE, NELSON HUSKISSON CANADA, BROCKLEBANK, and ALEXANDRA	9ᴰ	1/6
GLADSTONE **SEAFORTH SANDS**	6ᴰ	1/-

The issuing of Through Tickets is subject to the conditions and regulations referred to in the Time Tables, Bills, and Notices of the respective Companies on whose Railways, Coaches or Steamboats they are available, and the holder, by accepting a Through Ticket agrees that the respective Companies are not to be liable for any loss or damage, injury, delay or detention arising off these several Railways, Coaches or Steamboats. The Contract and liability of each Company are limited to its own Railway, Coaches or Steamboats.

Hargreaves Building,
5. **Chapel Street, Liverpool, 3.**
March, 1955.

H. MAXWELL ROSTRON,
General Manager & Engineer

An L.O.R. train in strange company at Aintree on "Grand National" day in 1956. The "Overhead" train on the special race day working stands next to a main-line special train.

Photo R. Stephens.

Closure and Demolition.

The main-line railways of the country were Nationalised on 1st January, 1948, but the Liverpool Overhead Railway carried on serving the city as it had done since the day it was opened back in 1893, age, war-weariness and depreciation notwithstanding. The railway's patrons and wellwishers were however, blissfully unaware of what was happening within the offices of the company in Hargreaves Building, that ancient and soot-blackened edifice in Chapel Street within sight and sound of the railway and river. From that sanctum was to come an announcement that shattered complacency in one resounding blow!

One snow-slushed gray, miserable day in February, 1955, bold headlines in the evening papers proclaimed black news — the possibility that the famous "Dockers Umbrella" might soon cease to exist! Many people however, thought this was an unseemly joke — "They just won't close *this* railway" was the cry — "It just can't happen". One elderly, retired engineer who had watched the railway being built said "Let them stop the trains for just one day and there will be anarchy on the docks". "After all", people said, "who in their right mind would even remotely contemplate the closure of a vital and busy railway", one that had moreover, carried nine-million passengers the previous year. Facts were hard however, even if unbelievable. The company, anxious about the condition of the structure after more than 60 years of service had lately called in consulting engineers to carry out a thorough examination. They reported that, among other things, the arched decking plates would need to be renewed within five years, and the cost of this work was estimated to be in the region of two-million pounds, a sum that was far beyond the resources of the company already struggling against many adverse factors. They were left no alternative but to consider closing the railway. The decision was not made lightly, as the Liverpool Overhead Railway Company were a proud body with a long record of service second to none, and the prospect of Liverpool without the "Overhead" pained them as well as the customers.

As soon as the threat of closure struck home, it was hailed as an outrage that must be stopped, and a long series of public meetings was begun, the first being held in no less regal surroundings than the Concert Room of St. George's Hall, this meeting being attended by the Chairman of the railway company and the leader of the City Council, also various other municipal officials, councillors, and trades union representatives. The object of this and subsequent meetings was to try and find a way of saving the railway by municipalisation, nationalisation or local financial aid. Local authorities and trades unions threw their weight into the battle and so many friends and supporters did the railway have that its future as a going concern seemed assured. The correspondence columns in the local press were full of pleas to save the "Overhead" and numerous suggestions were made on how this could be accomplished. The "Evening Express" conducted a ballot, which resulted in an overwhelming majority vote to keep the railway open. As time went on however, hopes began to fade. Neither the Liverpool Corporation nor the Mersey Docks & Harbour Board were willing to take the railway over completely, and although a number of bodies offered to help financially, agreement could not be reached on the degree of aid that each should provide. The company offered to keep the railway intact (though not operating) for a period of nine months after the closure date and to postpone winding up the organisation until that amount of time had elapsed to enable further studies of the situation to be made and to give any outside body that might have a successful plan for saving the railway to put such into force. It was no use however, as disharmony and disagreement developed and the doom of the "Overhead" was irrevocably sealed. Late in 1956 the closure notices were pasted up on station hoardings by saddened station staff and the dock workers read them, convinced at last that they would need to find alternative transport, and awaited the end with trepidation.

There was much sanctimonious hypocrisy and widespread shedding of crocodile tears after this ignominious failure to save the railway. It was incredible that the huge efforts made over many months had come to nought. The fact that politics were involved however, meant that little hope of success could really be entertained, and this was fully borne out in due course. It was stated by one prominent member of the Liverpool council that the land occupied by the railway was needed for other purposes, but as events have turned out, only a very small amount of such land has been built upon or otherwise made use of. Excuses for failure just had to be found! Hard feelings there were in plenty about the closure of the Overhead Railway, but nobody at the time could forsee what was to happen to Liverpool's dockland over the following 20 years, which would have affected the line to a considerable extent. This will be referred to again later.

The last few weeks of operation saw many visitors arrive for a last ride on the railway while the opportunity still offered, and the number of empty film cartons lying around was testimony enough to the amount of photography carried out to preserve the record of the line. One encountered photographers at every station and vantage point along the way. As the final week of operation wore on, interupted by the Christmas holidays, the gloom deepened in the hearts of the railway's many devotees. At last came the cold, dark night of Sunday, 30th December, 1956, a night that marked the end of an era in the transport history of Merseyside. Numbers of people left their warm firesides and made their various ways to the Pier Head to travel for the last time on the trains that were so familiar, and which it was hard to believe, would not be out as usual on the morrow to carry the crowds to work. A few hardy optimists considered the shut-down as temporary however, and confidently predicted an early re-opening. Alas for dreams!

The last Up train left Seaforth & Litherland station bound for Dingle at 10.03 PM, formed of original rolling stock, which was fitting for the occasion. In the opposite direction a rebuilt train left Dingle for Seaforth Sands, also at 10.03 PM, so that one of the oldest and one of the newest trains performed the last runs. They were timed to pass at Pier Head station, which they did amid a fusilade of loud reports from fog detonators which had been placed on the rails, possibly the first time such things had ever been used on this line of automatic signals? At each station at which the trains called (some were closed as it was Sunday) people were waiting to witness the departure or to board for the remaining part of the journey. Little groups stood in the chill wind at street corners and gave farewell waves as the last trains rumbled by. The collector shoes struck vivid blue flashes from the soon to be de-energised live rails and the colour-light signals, about to be extinguished for ever, shone brilliantly in the darkness. The Up train from Seaforth to Dingle carried the most passengers and there were few spare seats. In any case, passengers mostly stood in groups, chatting about old times on the railway or possible future prospects, and there was constant movement of people to and fro in each carriage. At one station in Bootle, several girls got in and sat in a group at one end of the carriage. They started to sing sentimental songs, but very soon lapsed into silence — some of them were employees of the railway and the realisation struck them that this was the final end and that they would not be turning out next day to open the stations for business as they had been doing for so long. Station cats were handed in through the windows en-route to new abodes, and at several places high-pitched shrieks of salutation from the whistles of Mersey Docks & Harbour Board locomotives being steamed for the next days work rent the cold night air. Some ships sirens did likewise in final salute as the familiar trains rumbled by for the last time.

When the last Up train finally arrived at Dingle there was a considerable crowd on the platform to meet it. The passengers left the carriages and mingled with the throng, and a marked reluctance on the part of everybody to leave the station was noticeable. Even the staff were in no hurry to go home on this eventful night; employees and public stayed to talk, reminisce and express hopes. A strong rumour was abroad that fresh attempts had been made to save the railway and that a further meeting of interested parties was to be held in the near future, and with this slight raising of the spirits people drifted off homewards at a late hour. The station inspector, after getting in touch with Seaforth Sands by telephone to ascertain that the last Down train had safely arrived, pulled over the main switch that cut-off the electric current and extinguished the signal lights. The Liverpool Overhead Railway was now dead — only the burial now remained to be carried out. This was the longest night, and what followed was merely a long drawn-out interment.

Next morning, Monday, the current was switched on again and a staff train ran from Dingle to Seaforth Sands at 8.45 AM to carry the few persons concerned with the dismemberment of the railway. Another train was operated in the late afternoon, but for the railway's regular patrons it was the unfamiliar experience of riding to work in buses, the first ones to run along the dock road since the horse-drawn conveyances of 60 years previously. The Liverpool Corporation Passenger Transport Department had undertaken to provide services in place of the trains, a total of 44 buses being required, a figure later reduced however, as many of the former regular train passengers did not use the buses for one reason or another.

There were several trains at the Dingle end of the line at the time of closure, and during the ensuing months they were driven to Seaforth Sands to join the remainder, one set hauling another so that the men could ride back directly instead of using the bus! These "ghost" trains aroused a great deal of interest and some slight optimism, a few people thinking that the railway had reopened! The trains were left on the structure in a continuous line that stretched from Seaforth Sands almost to Gladstone Dock station, and were eventually broken up, or the carriage bodies sold for use as sheds. The stations and the now silent, deserted structure quickly assumed a derelict and woebegone appearance due to the effects of disuse, the weather and continuous attack by young vandals and unscrupulous collectors of scrap metal. On 25th February, 1957, the promised meeting took place but achieved nothing, and in view of the quickening deterioration of the structure the company decided to have it demolished as soon as possible. The contract for this work was awarded to George Cohen, Sons & Company Ltd.

The demolition men with their cranes and burners duly moved in, and on 23rd September, 1957 the first section was sliced through and removed at a point near the Herculaneum Dock. The work then progressed steadily towards Seaforth Sands and, as in the days of construction, no interference with dock traffic was allowed, but all problems were solved and no hold-ups occured. The bowstring girder-bridges posed the trickiest problems and were left until the last — they stood in isolation supported on old up-ended boilers until the work of dismantling them could be tackled, which it was, on Sundays, when traffic on the city streets was fairly light. By the end of January, 1958 the "Dockers Umbrella" was, like the sails of the ships it knew in its youth, finally furled. Expensive works including resurfacing of the dock road and pavements had to be performed after the railway had closed — a bus ride on the old setted surface was a bone-shaking experience.

As the dock worker stands at the roadside waiting for a bus, especially when it is cold and wet, he might well recall the days when he waited in shelter during bad weather or enjoyed cool Summer breezes high above the fume-laden street. There is nothing now to remind him of his erstwhile "umbrella". Time passes and memories fade, but even nowadays, mention of the Overhead Railway arouses emotions, nostalgic and otherwise. Some people even think that a new one should be built! A new structure might be made eventually, but it will be probably a concrete one for motor vehicles, several times as wide and hugely more expensive, to carry the equivalent passenger traffic of the former railway. So far as tourist traffic is concerned, the sight-seers no longer come to the docks in large numbers as they did in railway days, as it is not possible to see anything of ships or docks from the buses and even so, these vehicles do not follow the entire length of the dock road as the railway did. There was however, a city bus tour operated for some years (during the Summer) which took in part of the dock estate, successor to a joint bus and train tour, using the Overhead Railway, which was operated before the line closed. The dock workers do not all travel by bus nowadays as motor coaches and other vehicles owned by contractors and various firms are used to take men to their different jobs and localities along the docks, and many travel to and from work in their own cars.

Even in the last days of the Overhead Railway special trains were run for visiting parties. For instance, on a day in May, 1956 a total of 20 such trains was operated, for people who had come from Nottingham, Bradford, Manchester, Stockport, Birmingham, Crewe, Brighouse, Sheffield and Derby. Large numbers of visitors travelled on the service trains too.

On walking along the dock road today it is difficult to realise that the Overhead Railway ever existed until one discovers a surviving column sunk into the wall of a dockside shed, or some other rare trace. Until early in 1966 a couple of short lengths of the structure were in use carrying a steam-main from Clarence Dock power station to industrial plants in the vicinity of Waterloo Dock, but certainly little else remains. The site of the station at Seaforth Sands has altered completely, the erstwhile carriage shed and works, given over to other uses after closure of the railway, were demolished in 1969 and the land they occupied used as a storage ground for containers in connection with the Gladstone Dock container terminal. Extensive road works and demolitions have completely altered the character of the district surrounding the former station since 1956.

Dingle tunnel, its portal still bearing the inscription "LO RLY SOUTHERN EXTENSION 1896" still gapes incongruously in the rock face above the railway tracks at Herculaneum Dock, and the former station in Park Road is now something quite different. Only in the County Museum is it possible to see anything to remind people that there was such a railway as the Liverpool Overhead, in the shape of carriage No.3, which after many years standing in the open at North Mersey goods yard and later at Breck Road sidings, was fully restored and is now one of the most valuable exhibits in the museum transport gallery. Children unborn when the Overhead Railway was in operation can sit on the same wooden seats that accommodated their grandfathers, but can never experience the pleasure of riding along 16 feet above the dock road on one of the World's most fascinating train journeys. In addition to the carriage, the museum has a number of photographs, tickets, posters and other "Overhead" memorabilla, whilst an authoritative history of the line was written by Mr. Charles E. Box, son of a former LOR General Manager. More recently, the museum authorities have issued a facsimile of an early Overhead Railway pictorial poster showing a river full of ships — a sight now almost forgotten!

Things have of course, changed along the docks since the Overhead Railway passed away. Ships no longer come to Liverpool in the numbers they once did, the great passenger liners have gone and the dock labour forces are much reduced from their former strength due partly to less trade, mechanisation, and containerisation of freight. The South Docks have closed completely whilst most of the main-line goods stations have closed too. Even had the railway survived, what would its position be in the early 1980's? The dock road buses do only moderate business except in the peak hours and it is likely that the same would have applied to the trains had they continued to run. Perhaps however, the railway might have been upgraded and used as a link between the ex- L & Y and CLC main-line systems as was proposed in the early 1900's, a function which today is provided by the new underground Link Line which connects North and South Liverpool as the LOR did. However, the latter line, being tied to the dock road would have proved far less convenient than the underground system. Perhaps latter-day factors would have killed the "Overhead" eventually, even had it survived the crises of the 1950's.

Derelict L.O.R. trains and demolition work in progress at Seaforth Sands in July, 1957. The long-familiar floating crane "Mammoth" looms in the background.

Photo J. Maher.

The "last round-up". L.O.R. trains awaiting breaking-up at Seaforth Sands. July, 1957.

Photo J. Maher.

Seagulls hover and perch upon the "bones" of the dead and disappearing Overhead Railway structure at Princes Dock in the Summer of 1958.

Photo J.B. Horne.

Photo J.B. Horne.

Looking down the "switchback" at Bramley-Moore Dock on a murky day in 1957, after closure of the railway. Clarence Dock Power Station chimneys - the "ugly sisters", smoke driven by the South-Westerly wind, form a dramatic background.

A Hunslet 0-6-0 Saddle Tank locomotive engaged on demolition work on the L.O.R. Seen near Seaforth Sands, having just delivered a train of scrap rails for removal by British Railways.

Photo J.B. Horne.

The dawn of a new era. A Liverpool Corporation bus en route to Dingle on the L.O.R. replacement service, on its first day of operation, Monday 31st December, 1956.

Photo H. Haddrill.

Steam Locomotives.

We have already noted that steam locomotives were ruled out for working the trains on the Liverpool Overhead Railway, but the company did employ one such machine. This was a tiny 0-4-0 Well Tank, built in 1893 by the famous manufacturer's, Kitsons of Leeds. The engine did not carry any number or nameplates, but was known throughout the staff as "Lively Polly". It was used by the Engineering Department for construction and permanent-way trains, hauling materials on flat wagons mounted on carriage bogies. "Lively Polly" was normally housed in a small shed at Seaforth Sands, where it was a familiar sight for many years. On icy Winter nights hardy men turned out with the engine to patrol the line breaking ice off the live rail by means of special scrapers fitted to the engine for the purpose, which in appearance resembled the collector shoes of an electric train. With such fittings the little locomotive looked for all the world as though in similar fashion to its passenger-carrying colleagues, it was electrically propelled, until it started off with the familiar exhaust sounds that belong to steam engines alone. The old engine was replaced in 1947 by a less romantic four-wheeled diesel machine of Ruston & Hornsby manufacture. This was not the end for "Lively Polly" however, as, having eventually been sold to Messrs Rea Ltd., she was sent in 1948 to Monks Ferry coal wharf in Birkenhead, and for 12 years worked hard in shifting wagons loaded with coal destined for burning in Mersey tug steamers. This was in great contrast to the long, leisurely life of her LOR years, and it speaks well for steam engines in general that such an ancient machine could accomplish such work day-in and day-out so late in its life. By the latter end of the 1950's many of the tug boats had been converted to burn oil fuel, whilst new ones were diesel propelled, so work at Monks Ferry ceased and "Lively Polly" was broken up for scrap. This was a pity because no other example of the type survives, which was rare in any case as only a few examples were built.

During demolition of the Overhead Railway at least two steam locomotives were employed on the haulage of recovered rails and other materials, that were loaded onto bogie bolster wagons hired from British Railways, and these were the first main-line goods vehicles to venture onto the LOR. The first engine to appear was an 0-4-0 Saddle Tank built by Hudswell Clarke of Leeds in 1893 (the year the LOR was opened). Next came a modern 0-6-0 Saddle Tank by the Hunslet Engine Company, also of Leeds, of a class familiar on the Mersey Dock lines. This had the number 600 boldly displayed on its tanks. These locomotives certainly looked strange and out of place up on the structure, and excited a great deal of interest and comment. For a short time an old steam crane shorn of its jib did duty as a locomotive!

"Lively Polly", the only steam locomotive owned by the Liverpool Overhead Railway Company. Photographed at Monk's Ferry wharf in 1956. Photo J.B. Horne.

Final Thoughts.

There was of course, much more to the Liverpool Overhead Railway than this all too brief survey has covered. It was a railway of great character that traversed an area of intense industry and a certain amount of squalor, over which hung a perpetual smoky haze, numerous odours and scents. The railway was scorched by the sun in Summer, and in Winter was often obscured by fog or covered with snow. Chill winds and blustery gales whistled through its girders. Gangs of children wandered along the dock road beneath it, and it was visible at the foot of every street that led to the river front and docks. The station staff were used to meeting men from virtually every land on this earth, and during the war American servicemen were reminded of New York or Chicago by it. Students of rail transportation came from far and wide to see it, and in its time it had distinguished visitors — King Feisal of Iraq, G.K. Chesterton, Rudyard Kipling, whilst the poet John Betjeman was one of its numerous devotees. Finally, we recall how the trains kept going on Winter days of fog and ice when traffic below it on the dock road was hindered. We see in the mind's eye cold, dark mornings, dock workers crowding into the trains before eight o'clock, dumping haversacks and bags of tools on the floor, smoking or reading the paper, exchanging witticisms and in season, discussing the football results, or on Summer mornings when the sun was up before the first train of the day moved off, clear blue skies over the Mersey estuary and the industrial haze only just beginning to spread, the smoke plumes from chimneys drifting away on the breeze. The Overhead Railway has vanished — almost without trace, but it will be a long time yet before it fades from the memories of the people who knew it during the years of ceaseless service to the city that could not save it from destruction. The railway has become legendary since the wheels of its rumbling trains came to a final halt on that dark night more than two and-a-half decades ago.

LIVERPOOL OVERHEAD RAILWAY.

ONE DOG (Accompanied by Passenger)

Toxteth Dock (L.O.R.) to

on the V.C.R.Ly.

FARE

This Ticket, which is available for a single journey only, must be given up at destination Station.

00209

L.O.R. 1st SINGLE
For conditions see back
James Street (A) TO
HUSKISSON
or any inter. Station
Fare 3½d.
I S 11
HUSKISSON

5680

L.O.R. 1st SINGLE
For conditions see back
James Street (A) TO
HUSKISSON
or any inter. Station
Fare 3½d.
I S 11
HUSKISSON

5680

L.O.R.
EARLY MORNING RETURN 3rd
For conditions see back
(Series K)
Seaforth Sands TO
JAMES STREET
Fare 9½d.

0873

L.O.R.
EARLY MORNING RETURN 3rd
For conditions see back
(Series K)
James Street TO
SEAFORTH SANDS
Fare 9½d.

0873

(B) L.O.R.
For conditions see back
Canada TO
BROCKLEBANK
or any inter. Station
available for one journey on day of
issue or following day
Third Class / 3 R. 4
CANADA

5598

L.O.R. (B)
For conditions see back
Brocklebank TO
CANADA
or any inter. Station
Third Class
Fare 3d.

7598

L.O.R.
WORKMAN'S TICKET
THIRD CLASS
Issued subject to the
Company's Bye-Laws and
Regulations and Condi-
tions in the Time Tables,
Bills and Notices
Canada to
NELSON

3736

L.O.R.
WORKMAN'S TICKET
THIRD CLASS
Issued subject to the
Company's Bye-Laws and
Regulations and Condi-
tions in the Time Tables,
Bills and Notices
to
CANADA
Fare 3d.

3736

L.O.R.
Not Transferable. This ticket is issued subject to the
General Notices, Regulations & Conditions in the Co.'s
current time tables. Available on day of issue only.
THIRD CLASS
NELSON L.O.R. TO
WATERLOO L.M.S.
Waterloo L.M.S. Fare 6d

0492

0492

RETURN M T W T F S
WEEKLY THIRD CLASS
L. W. R.
Expiring on Saturday following date of issue.
DINGLE to
SEAFORTH SANDS & BACK
Available for One Journey each way the Outward
by train leaving the starting point up to 8.30 a.m
and the Return Journey by any train each day.
Fare 4s.5d.
OUTWARD M T W T F S

2737

L.O.R.
FOR CONDITIONS SEE BACK
SEAFORTH S'DS TO
TOXTETH
or any intermediate Stn
on day of issue or follow
ing day.
First Class / 1 R. 15
SEAFORTH S'DS

7667

L.O.R.
FOR CONDITIONS SEE BACK
TOXTETH TO
SEAFORTH S'DS
or any intermediate Stn
First Class
Fare 1s.4d.

7667

Tickets Please.

When you booked your journey on the Liverpool Overhead Railway you were provided with a substantial pasteboard ticket of the standard Edmondson card type, which was issued in the time-honoured manner from a rack, then stamped on an old-fashioned ticket dating press. There were no flimsy pieces of paper or economy versions — the tickets were solid and durable so that they were not easily rolled or screwed-up as was the case with local tram and bus tickets, and they had to be given up at the passenger's destination station.

In addition to ordinary Single and Return tickets for First and Third Class travel, the company provided quite an astonishing number of journey classifications. There were tickets for workmen, for early morning journeys, evening trips, day trips, round trips, excursions, and through tickets to stations on the LMS Wirral and Southport lines. Combined Ribble Motor Services and LOR tickets were available for a time, and also through tickets from LOR stations to Wirral destinations via the Mersey ferries and Birkenhead Corporation Tramways. Dog, bicycle and Privilege tickets were also of the same style as the ordinary issues, but season tickets were larger and of distinctive shape. Altogether the variety was considerable for a railway only seven miles long and with only one route. The colours too, were in great variety.

The stations on the line were numbered from 1 to 17, and the number of the issuing station was overprinted in large size on the face of each ticket. In the case of return tickets, the numbers of both the issuing and destination stations was shown on the respective outward and inward portions. This scheme speeded-up ticket checking because the ticket collector could see at a glance if a particular ticket was valid for the section of line travelled upon. The only exception to the numbering rule was Seaforth & Litherland station which although served by Overhead trains, was not owned by the company — it was originally an L & Y station which passed to the LMS, and later British Railways. Each LOR station had a turnstile adjacent to the booking office (with the exception of Pier Head, Dingle and Seaforth Sands at which the booking offices were at street level, the turnstiles being on the platforms) so that nobody was able to get on a train without a ticket.

During the "Blitz" period of the 1939 War, buses were used to cover gaps in the LOR structure due to bomb damage. Ordinary bus type tickets were issued by the conductors on these vehicles. There were no excursion, cheap day and round-trip tickets issued during the war years, of course.

Large numbers of Liverpool Overhead Railway tickets have survived in private collections, and upon looking through them one can become so absorbed as to feel that the railway is still in being, but if it no longer exists in a tangible form, its memorabilia helps to re-create something of the atmosphere of that unique line along the docks of Liverpool and Bootle.

Publicity.

Although the Liverpool Overhead Railway was built primarily to transport passengers engaged on business along the line of docks, the company soon realised that the superb views from the trains offered a potential for tourist traffic at week-ends and during holiday times, and they set about attracting sight-seers by advertising and publicity. Posters depicting the River Mersey crowded with shipping were produced prior to the Great War of 1914, and an example of one of these has been reproduced for sale by the Merseyside County Museums. The poster is somewhat inaccurate however in its portrayal of the actual railway and train, but puts over the scenic aspect very well indeed.

During the 1930's two very colourful though technically inaccurate posters appeared, showing busy docks and shipping, with a River Mersey of Mediterranean blue! Another poster, of cartoon character was displayed for some years showing a large driver's head looking out of the driving compartment windows, with the caption "See the Dox".

The object of these colourful posters was to encourage people to view the docks and shipping, for which the railway provided the very best vantage points as the line ran close to the docks for almost its entire length. It was a train ride remembered with excitement by all who took the poster's advice and booked a Round-Trip ticket (which included a permit to go aboard certain ocean liners until the war put a stop to the practice). The almost empty River Mersey of today makes the scenes shown on the Overhead Railway posters seem almost legendary!

Handbills advertising through bookings at cheap fares between LOR and LMS stations, particularly Southport and Wirral resorts were published for many years, whilst each year the special train service between Dingle and Aintree for the "Grand National" was given wide publicity.

During the 1930's the Liverpool Overhead Railway Company produced a useful guide with a folding map of the line and docks which was also illustrated with shipping and dockland scenes. There was no tourist travel encouraged during the war years (1939-45), but a new, much thinner and abbreviated two-page guide appeared thereafter. Nowadays these guides are valued collector's items.

Each successive edition of the Liverpool Official Handbook contained a description of the Overhead Railway and its facilties, whilst an advertisement for the line was also included. The railway received mention in numerous publications relating to Liverpool, as it was one of the city's chief attractions, the passing of which isolated the people from the shipping as the dockland scene could not be savoured in any better way than by a ride on the "Overhead".

The 25th Anniversary of the closure of the Liverpool Overhead Railway was commemorated by the Merseyside Philatelic Society, which produced a special cover on which is depicted a profile view of one of the railway's characteristic carriages. A card featuring one of the colourful LOR posters was also produced by the Society.

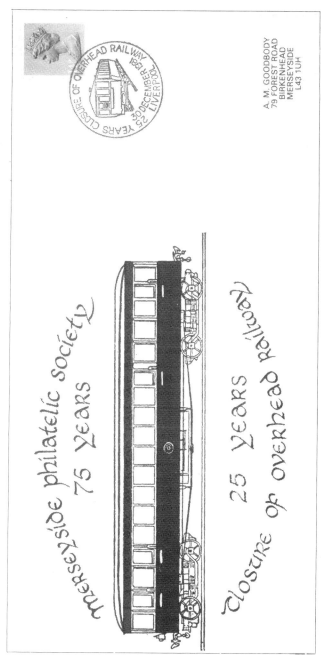

Merseyside philatelic society
75 years

25 years
closure of overhead railway

A. M. GOODBODY
79 FOREST ROAD
BIRKENHEAD
MERSEYSIDE
L43 1UH

ACKNOWLEDGEMENTS

The following sources of reference were found useful in the preparation of this book: Liverpool Evening Express; "The Liverpool Overhead Railway" by C.E. Box; Liverpool Overhead Railway Company publicity; "Recollections of a Busy Life" by Sir W.B. Forwood. Cuttings from various engineering journals in the City Record Office were also a useful source of information. For the provision of illustrations I am indebted to Norman Forbes, Harry Haddrill, John Horne, John Maher, the late Robert B. Parr, John A. Senior and Ron Stephens, whilst some are my own. Permission to reproduce the map of the system was kindly granted by Mr. J.N. Slater, Editor of the "Railway Magazine". Grateful thanks also to Patricia Shimmin for her voluntary assistance in typing a great deal of railway material for this and (hopefully) further books on the railways of Merseyside.